w

CHARISMATIC SPIRITUALITY

Charismatic Spirituality

STEPHEN B. CLARK

PUBLISHED BY ST. ANTHONY MESSENGER PRESS
CINCINNATI, OHIO

Servant Books is an imprint of St. Anthony Messenger Press.

Scripture passages have been taken from the Revised Standard Version, Catholic edition. Copyright 1946, 1952, 1971 by the Division of Christian Education of the National Council of Churches of Christ in the USA. Used by permission.

Published by St. Anthony Messenger Press
28 W. Liberty Street
Cincinnati, OH 45202-6498
www.AmericanCatholic.org

Book design by Sandy L. Digman

04 05 06 10 9 8 7 6 5 4 3 2 1

Printed in the United States of America
ISBN 1-56955-390-4

LIBRARY OF CONGRESS CATALOGING-IN-PUBLICATION DATA

CLARK, STEPHEN B.
  CHARISMATIC SPIRITUALITY / STEPHEN B. CLARK.
     P. CM.
  ISBN 1-56955-390-4 (ALK. PAPER)
  1. PENTECOSTALISM. 2. SPIRITUAL LIFE—CHRISTIANITY. I. TITLE.
  BR1644.C527 2004
  248.4—DC22
                          2004001587

CONTENTS

Introduction

In our times the work of the Holy Spirit has become a notable center of attention. This has partly occurred because of the Pentecostal movement and the charismatic renewal, but the concern has extended into most sectors of the Christian people.

Many explanations for this have been given. Perhaps the most compelling is connected to the weakening of the institutional and societal or cultural supports for Christian life due to the changes in modern society. As a result of this change in the societal status of Christianity, many Christians are looking to the Lord in a new way. They want him to reestablish his people and give them a renewed, spiritually stronger foundation through the work of the Holy Spirit.

"The work of the Holy Spirit" is a phrase that simply means "what the Holy Spirit does." It is commonly used to refer to what he does in the redemption of the human race by making it possible for people to live the life God intends for them, rather than what he did to create the world (Gn 1:2) and to sustain it (Ps 104:27-30). It primarily refers, then, to what he does in human beings who have faith in Christ. The Holy Spirit is God himself, entering into human life and enabling human beings who believe the gospel to live in a way that they could not live by their own power. Those who have the Holy Spirit at work in them can have true spiritual life.

"Spiritual life" can be understood in a New Age way as well as in a primarily psychological way (for example, "Jungian spirituality"). In both these meanings, it refers to a life that human beings can attain by realizing certain powers latent in themselves. However, when we say here "spiritual life," or "life of the Spirit," we mean the life that is produced by the Holy Spirit working in us. In order to realize the full benefits of that life, we need to have a charismatic spirituality.

We now are heirs to a certain use of the word *charismatic*. It refers to whatever people think of as connected to the charismatic movement or charismatic renewal—good, bad, and indifferent. Those of us who were involved in the beginnings of the charismatic renewal, however, did not think of ourselves as beginning a movement. Rather, we simply believed that we were rediscovering the work of the Holy Spirit in a new way, one that allowed us to experience results we had not experienced previously. That rediscovery was centered around what was called "expectant faith," the faith that the Lord will do what he says he will do—and what he did for the first Christians— if we take him at his word.

Probably everyone familiar with the charismatic renewal movement would agree that it has been concerned with "baptism in the Spirit" and "spiritual gifts." In the early days of the movement, these were the two most common topics of discussion and seemed to define the renewal itself. But there is a more helpful way of defining "charismatic renewal." "Charismatic renewal" is best understood as a renewal in the work of the Holy Spirit. That work includes baptism in the Spirit and spiritual gifts, but these can only be understood well in the context of the complete work of the Holy Spirit. They are not supposed to stand out by themselves.

The word *renewal* is a very important part of the phrase "charismatic renewal." A renewal is intended to renew—bring to new life—an aspect of Christianity, not to add something to Christianity. A charismatic renewal, then, if it is a true renewal, should not be intended to promote Christianity plus something else (like charismatic experience). Nor is a renewal intended to create a special group of Christians (the charismatics, the spiritual ones). Rather it should renew something all Christians should have. In the case of charismatic renewal, it is the work of the Holy Spirit that is to be renewed in all.

This is not a book on the charismatic movement or its history. Nor is this a book on baptism of the Spirit and spiritual gifts. I have written books that treat those topics, but they are not the primary focus here. This is a book on charismatic spirituality—how to approach daily life, how to live as a Christian, if we wish to benefit from the work of the Holy Spirit in us.

Spirituality can be understood as referring just to prayer life or piety. It is here used, however, in a somewhat different way. People often talk about evangelical spirituality or Benedictine spirituality and mean something more than the prayer life or piety of evangelicals or Benedictines. They are referring to their approach to all of Christian life. Spirituality is being used in this book in such a broader sense. Charismatic spirituality, then, is the approach to Christian life of someone who has experienced a renewal in the work of the Holy Spirit and has responded to that renewal in a way that has made it a source of more effective Christian living.

If the work of the Holy Spirit is something for all Christians—and who can deny that it is—charismatic spirituality is something for all Christians. This book is written in that conviction. However, there are also special emphases that those who are now called charismatics exhibit, as well as special practices, and even styles of doing things associated with the movement. The last chapter of this book will try to sort out some of the questions that arise from such practices. Most of the book, however, simply considers truths and practices that should be the same for all Christians.

Charismatic spirituality can be summarized in terms of five main features. Each of these will be the subject of one of the chapters of the book. They are as follows:

1. Charismatic spirituality is based on the understanding that the gift of the Holy Spirit is the specific newness of the new covenant (the gift or grace Christ came to bring) and should be experienced as the basis of a new relationship with God.

2. Charismatic spirituality should help us be spiritual(ized) people, people who love God and love their neighbor and are enabled to do so because they have an experiential relationship with God.

3. Charismatic spirituality is based upon confidence that the Holy Spirit in us transforms, enlightens, and strengthens us so that we can be spiritual(ized) people.

4. Charismatic spirituality is based on the conviction that God acts in our world to make Christians effective in their service of him, without implying that (spiritualized) natural means are worthless or unimportant.

5. Charismatic spirituality involves approaching particular areas of Christian life, like prayer and worship or evangelism, by expecting the Holy Spirit to make direct, experiential contact for us with God so that we might receive personal spiritual strength and added light and power, including gifts and graces, to act effectively in that area.

There are many more Scripture passages that could be added to the ones cited in this book. At the end there is a survey of the passages that speak about the work of the Holy Spirit in Scripture. They can be used for further study or just to see where the points made here are further substantiated in Scripture.

This book is intended to be ecumenically accessible. All orthodox Christians—Orthodox, Catholic, and Protestant alike—understand the work of the Holy Spirit the same way. The only ecumenical differences relevant to this topic come from the controversies over the Pentecostal movement early in the twentieth century. At that time some conservative evangelicals denied the possibility of spiritual gifts after the close of the New Testament, while some Pentecostal churches made tongues the initial evidence of the Holy Spirit's work a matter of church doctrine. The question of the initial evidence does not come up in this book. Those who do not accept the possibility of spiritual gifts now will not agree with parts of this book, but apart from that this book should be acceptable to all orthodox Christians. Thus it is written in a vocabulary and style that hopefully will be accessible to all.

CHAPTER ONE

The Grace of Pentecost

We are going to begin by asking what happened to the human race on the day of Pentecost. People often speak about "the grace of Pentecost," and by that they mean the gift or grace that was given to the human race on that day. Pentecost is the day that completed the establishment of the new covenant, because Pentecost is the day on which God gave the gift that made possible the new covenant relationship with him. Of course, Pentecost was the day on which the Holy Spirit "was given" (Jn 7:39) or was "poured out" (Acts 2:33), so the grace of Pentecost is the result of the outpouring of the Holy Spirit.

In this chapter we will mainly look at the scriptural teaching on Pentecost and the giving or outpouring of the Spirit that occurred then. That means that we will primarily consider Acts 2, the New Testament passage where Pentecost is described. But, surprising as it may be to some, Pentecost is not just a feast talked about in the New Testament; it was instituted in the Old Testament. In fact, it is only a Christian or new covenant feast because the new covenant is built upon the old and fulfills what is in the old, including its feasts. We will therefore begin with what the old covenant tells us about the Feast of Pentecost.

The Day of Pentecost on Sinai

Most of us can look through the whole Old Testament in the Bible we normally use and not find any references to Pentecost. That is one of the reasons why we are surprised at the idea that Pentecost is an old covenant feast. But it is mentioned somewhat often in the Old Testament under the name of the Feast of Weeks. Pentecost means "fiftieth," and the day marks the festal conclusion to the week of weeks that made up Passover season (see Lv 23:15-16). Most English Bibles, following the Greek text, translate the name of the feast as "Pentecost" in the New Testament and, following the Hebrew, "the Feast of Weeks" in the Old Testament, but they are the same feast.

Pentecost was a harvest feast, the feast in which the first sheaf of the wheat harvest was offered to the Lord in thanksgiving for the harvest, acknowledging him as the giver of the harvest. At the time of Jesus and the apostles, however, it also seems to have been understood as the feast that celebrated the giving of the Law on Mount Sinai, which occurred about fifty days after the Exodus. That means that we can read about the first Day of Pentecost in Exodus 19 and 20. In doing that, we learn a great deal about the new covenant Day of Pentecost.

As we will see, it is important that the original Day of Pentecost occurred right after the Exodus. It is also significant that it occurred on the mountain of Sinai, which in Exodus 24 is called "the mountain of God." It was a mountain that belonged to God, one on which he was especially present. Mount Sinai, therefore, was a natural temple. The people of Israel were encamped before the place where the Lord was especially present.

Shortly after the people of Israel arrived, Moses "went up to the mountain," to the place of his special presence, as a priest would stand before the Holy of Holies in the temple. There

God spoke to him. He stated to Moses, and through him to the people of Israel, the purpose he had in redeeming them and bringing them to this place.

He began by saying, "You have seen what I did . . . , and how I . . . brought you to myself" (Ex 19:4). He, in other words, had delivered them, and they knew it. But he had not done that just to help out some poor needy group of slaves in trouble. He had delivered the descendants of Abraham, Isaac, and Jacob so that they could be with him, so that they could be his own people. To do that he was about to establish a covenant relationship with them.

God went on to speak about what he would do for them, but only "if you will obey my voice and keep my covenant" (Ex 19:5). There would be a condition, in other words. A covenant is something to be kept, something to be obeyed.

If the people of Israel kept that covenant, they would be "my own possession among all peoples" (Ex 19:5). They would be, in other words, a people in relationship with him, a people who would belong to him, his people among all others. The relationship he offered is analogous to the marriage relationship. Both are covenantal. He was saying, "I will be your God, and you will be my people" (see Jer 31:33; Ez 36:28), just as a man might say, "I will be your husband, and you will be my wife." He was offering this relationship to a people, not a group of individuals, although because the people is in a relationship with God, all the members are as well.

In describing the people they were to be, this new nation or kingdom, God spoke of "a kingdom of priests and a holy nation" (Ex 19:6). The Israelites would, in other words, be a people who would worship him, because they would know him for who he is and belong to him, their God. Worship is an expression of a true relationship with God.

Moses presented to the people what God had said to him. They responded, "Yes, we will accept the relationship the Lord is offering to us, and we will do all he tells us to do" (see Ex 19:8). Then the Lord told them that he would come to them and speak to them in person, not just through Moses.

On the appointed day God did manifest himself to the people to prepare them to hear what he had to say. But his manifestation was no everyday event. It began with thunders and lightnings, as if a violent storm were beginning, a common element in descriptions of awesome old covenant manifestations of God. There was also a very loud trumpet blast, like a call to arms or a reveille, so loud that the people were terrified. It was as if a bomb had gone off.

When Moses led the people out of the camp, a blazing fire was covering the mountain, giving off a cloud of smoke. Fire is a symbol of God and a common sign or manifestation of God's presence. Often, as here, the fire of God's presence is associated with a cloud. Although Sinai is not a volcano, it must have looked like a volcano that had just exploded, as it "burned with fire to the heart of heaven" (Dt 4:11). God had come down from his throne in heaven to Mount Sinai!

God then spoke to his people. The words he spoke were new to the people. They are, however, familiar to us, so familiar that we often do not realize their significance when we hear them. They were what the Israelites called "the ten words" (Dt 4:13, Hebrew) and what we call the Ten Commandments.

The Ten Commandments were the content of the covenant. We should be able to see that from Exodus 19 and 20. The people of Israel were to "obey his voice and keep his covenant." God, when he spoke from the cloud on Sinai, was telling them what that covenant was. The connection between the covenant and the commandments is even clearer in the description Moses gave on Mount Nebo of what had happened on Sinai:

"And he declared to you his covenant, which he commanded you to perform, that is, the ten commandments [words]; and he wrote them upon two tables [tablets] of stone" (Dt 4:13).

The Ten Commandments are often understood to be a summary of the moral law, and they are, but they were also the content of the covenant God gave to the people of Israel. They were, in other words, what God said the people of Israel needed to do to be in a good relationship with him. If they were going to live with him, this was the way they needed to live and so the way to live out the covenant. This was to be the response of the people to the fact that God had saved them, that he would save them again and again and would provide for them land, a place where they could have a good life.

Jesus summarized the Ten Commandments in two commandments, the commandments of love of God and love of neighbor (Mt 22:34-40). Using Jesus' summary, we could say that if the people of Israel were going to be a people who belonged to God, they needed to love him and love one another. Such a response allows the covenant relationship of God and his people to work well. They therefore needed to love God *and* those who were with them in relationship with God.

The commandments God gave were not just for special events, like gathering to meet God on Sinai or assembling to worship before the tent of meeting or the temple in Jerusalem. We might say they are not just for conferences or for church services and prayer meetings. "Thou shalt not kill" is not just a special instruction for how to spend Sunday. Nor does it mean "Thou shalt not kill the other people who are in church or the prayer meeting with you. You may kill them afterwards, but not while worshipping God." The instructions are for the whole of life, daily life, the way we live from morning to night, every day of every year. The Ten Commandments instruct us in a way of life, the way of life of a people who live in covenant with God.

On the Day of Pentecost at Sinai, then, God established a relationship with a people, the people of Israel. That relationship was covenantal and corporate, a committed relationship with a body of people. It involved how they lived their on-going daily life. This, then, is what God was about when he redeemed his people. Redemption is not an end in itself, but it is for a purpose. God redeems people so that they might come to him and live as his people. This was the purpose of the redemption that occurred at the Passover and in the Exodus. This, as we shall see, is the purpose of the redemption that occurs in the new covenant as well.

The Prophesied Renewal

Not all went well with the people of Israel, as anyone who has read much of the Old Testament knows. Some of what went wrong was normal sin, and that was provided for in the old covenant law. God did not expect his old covenant people to be flawless. However, during the last years of the Israelite monarchy they fell into ongoing syncretistic idolatry as a people, a sin so major that in God's eyes it amounted to national apostasy, rejection of him and the covenant he had made with them. As a result, the temple in Jerusalem was destroyed, and the bulk of the people were carried off into exile in Babylon. They were deprived of the land that was their inheritance and lived in a kind of slavery, similar to the slavery in Egypt from which they had been delivered.

During that time there were various prophecies about how God would restore his people. Several of them concerned an outpouring of God's Holy Spirit, which would renew the covenant relationship and so make it possible for the people to be what God had called them to be on the Day of Pentecost on Sinai. Two of them are particularly important for understanding the Day of Pentecost described in Acts 2. The first is a prophecy found in Ezekiel 36:26-28.

> A new heart I will give you, and a new spirit I will put within you; and I will take out of your flesh the heart of stone and give you a heart of flesh. And I will put my spirit within you, and cause you to walk in my statutes and be careful to observe my ordinances. You shall dwell in the land which I gave to your fathers; and you shall be my people, and I will be your God.

In the section before this, the prophecy spoke about God's gathering his people from all their places of exile and bringing them back to the Promised Land. It said that there he would cleanse them from their idolatry and other forms of uncleanness. When he did that, though, he would also change them interiorly. Their hearts and spirits, probably meaning their minds and wills, would be made new. They would no longer be rebellious, like stone in their resistance to obeying God, but would become obedient people who would keep his commandments. The covenant relationship would be renewed: "You shall be my people, and I will be your God."

There is one especially significant phrase in this prophecy. In promising that he would restore his people, the Lord said, "I will put my spirit within you." It would be the presence of his Spirit in them that would get them to obey him and keep his commandments. In other words, he would make an interior, personal change in them by putting his Spirit in them, and that is what would make the covenant relationship different, more successful.

The second prophecy is found Jeremiah 31:31-33. This prophecy was probably given a few years before that of Ezekiel.

> Behold, the days are coming, says the LORD, when I will make a new covenant with the house of Israel and the house of Judah, not like the covenant which I made with their fathers when I took them by the hand to bring them out of the land of Egypt, my covenant which they broke, though I was their husband,

> says the LORD. But this is the covenant which I will make with
> the house of Israel after those days, says the LORD: I will put my
> law within them, and I will write it upon their hearts; and I will
> be their God, and they shall be my people.

This prophecy is much like the one in Ezekiel. It promises the restoration of the covenant relationship established on Sinai, an effective restoration. The prophecy seems, in fact, to be speaking of the same event. But there are two phrases that are important to notice because they recur in the New Testament. The first is "new covenant." When God restores his people in the future, he will make a new covenant with them. The second is the phrase "I will write [my law] upon their hearts."

In other words, God was not going to do exactly what he had done before. On Sinai he had spoken the Ten Commandments to them, but then he had written them down on tablets of stone with his own hand so that his people could remember them and keep them. As a result, his people had to relate to God's law as something external to themselves, something they could read with their eyes or hear with their ears when it was spoken to them.

The new covenant, however, would be different. God would put his law inside of them. He himself would write it on their hearts—that is, put something inside of them that would make their minds interiorly know his law and incline their wills to do it. The prophecy in Ezekiel tells us what this is: the indwelling presence of God's Spirit.

These two passages indicate that God was going to restore his people. But they also indicate that in restoring them, he was going to do something more than he did when he made the covenant with them on Sinai. He would not abolish or cancel the covenant on Sinai, but fulfill it. In other words, he would do something that would effectively achieve the purpose he had in mind in giving the covenant of Sinai. He would do this through the presence of his Spirit inside of them, changing them interiorly.

There are other prophetic passages that concern the gift or outpouring of God's Spirit in the future. We will consider the most famous one, the prophecy in Joel, in the next section of this chapter when we look at Peter's speech in Acts 2. We will consider the prophecies in Isaiah about the outpouring of the Spirit in a later chapter. They all say much the same as the two prophecies we have looked at: The old covenant people of God can look to a day in the future when God will give them his Spirit as a way of fulfilling his purpose for them.

The Day of Pentecost on Mount Zion: Acts 2

For Christians, Pentecost commonly refers to the event that is described in the second chapter of the Book of Acts. It is the day on which the Holy Spirit was poured out upon the disciples of Jesus, fifty days after Jesus' resurrection. It is, in other words, the day referred to in John 7:39 in which the Holy Spirit was given, that is, was given in an abiding or ongoing way to human beings who had come to believe in Christ.

As we have seen, however, there were earlier Pentecosts, Feasts of Weeks, in which every year Jews offered the first fruits of the harvest. As we also have seen, at the time of Jesus the Jewish people seem to have celebrated the feast as the commemoration of the giving of the law on Mount Sinai, the first Day of Pentecost. It was on such a day that the Lord poured out the Holy Spirit upon Jewish believers in Christ. We could say *a priori* that the meaning of the outpouring of the Spirit was connected to the meaning of the feast on which Jesus determined it should happen. He chose that day to tell us something about the purpose for which he poured out the Spirit. If we also read the second chapter of Acts attentive to the Old Testament background, we will see many similarities to the description of the first Pentecost in Exodus 19 and Deuteronomy 4, enough that it seems clear that Luke intended us to see the Christian Pentecost as the fulfillment of the old covenant Pentecost.

As we have also seen, the old covenant Feast of Weeks or Pentecost was the celebration of the completion of the Passover season (the conclusion of the Fifty Days, in English commonly called Easter season). If Passover celebrated the deliverance from Egypt, then Pentecost, in celebrating the establishment of the covenant relationship between God and his people, was celebrating the completion of the deliverance from Egypt, that is, the accomplishment of the purpose for which God delivered his people. That also has a Christian significance.

English-speaking Christians often miss something about the connection between Easter and Pentecost, not only because English translations of the name of the Feast of Pentecost differ in the Old and New Testaments but also because we refer to the feast of Christ's resurrection as "Easter." In most other languages, including Greek, Christians refer to Easter as "Passover" (*pascha* in both Greek and Latin). That allows them to understand quickly that what they are celebrating at Easter is the new covenant Passover, the new covenant feast that fulfills the old covenant Passover.

The new covenant Passover is the feast that celebrates the death and resurrection of Christ. Just as the old covenant Passover celebrates the deliverance of God's people from bondage to Pharaoh in Egypt, so the new covenant Passover celebrates the deliverance of God's people from bondage to sin and Satan through the death of the true Passover Lamb, Christ, and his resurrection. The new covenant Pentecost celebrates the completion of the new covenant Passover by the outpouring of the Spirit. The outpouring of the Spirit, then, completed the establishing of the new covenant. The Feast of

Pentecost therefore celebrates the accomplishment of the purpose for which the Lord Jesus died and rose. This too we will see in Acts 2.

We will begin by looking at two sections of background from Acts 1, beginning with verses 4 and 5:

> And while staying with them he charged them not to depart from Jerusalem, but to wait for the promise of the Father, which, he said, "you heard from me, for John baptized with water, but before many days you shall be baptized with the Holy Spirit."

Chapter one of Acts begins with the risen Lord Jesus instructing his apostles. He included the command for them to wait in Jerusalem for the giving of what had been promised by the Father. Jerusalem was the place in which the temple was to be found, the special place of God's presence in the midst of his people. It was the city built on Mount Zion, the mountain that had replaced Mount Sinai as the chief place of God's presence on earth. The apostles were, in other words, to remain in what was the same "spiritual location" as were the Israelites when they were at Mount Sinai.

They were to wait there for *the* promise of the Father, the great gift that the Father had promised. As we have seen, the Old Testament prophecies spoke of a day in which the Lord would pour out his Spirit and in so doing create a new covenant relationship with himself, one that would be more spiritually effective. This outpouring of the Spirit was so much their hope that it could be called The Promise.

That hope had been stirred up by the preaching of John the Baptist. He had proclaimed a day of the coming of the Lord, a day of judgment soon to come, but he had also proclaimed a preliminary event: the baptism of the Holy Spirit. Those who had repented at his message would be immersed in the Holy Spirit, who would come upon them like water poured out from above and who would prepare them to undergo a time of spiritual conflict and judgment. John had also pointed out the baptizer, the Lord himself. Perhaps even more important than the fact that he would be the Lamb of God who would take away the sin of the world (Jn 1:29) was the fact that he would baptize them with the Holy Spirit and so bring about what his sacrificial death would make possible.

This background tells us a great deal about those who were gathered in Jerusalem in obedience to the Lord's command, the first candidates for baptism in the Spirit. They were already disciples, his followers. They believed in the Lord. They did not, however, just believe in Jesus as the Messiah sent by God to fulfill the prophecies about the son of David who would free his people. They also believed in the risen Son of God who had died for the sins of the world, who would come again to judge the living and the dead. They had just seen him.

In addition, as disciples were taught and were approved by the Lord, they were living lives of love of God and love of neighbor. They were keeping the commandments given on Sinai. Even more, they had been baptized with water. They still, however, missed something—something that would enable them to remain steadfast in the life they had been taught once the earthly presence of the Lord was taken away from them.

We can find other important background in the first chapter of Acts. The apostles returned from the Mount of Olives, the place of the ascension and the place where Jesus would come again, and they went to the Upper Room (Acts 1:12-13). The Upper Room was the place of the Last Supper or, as later Christians called it, the Lord's Supper or the Eucharist. There Jesus had begun the Passover, announcing to his disciples that he would be the Passover Lamb and fulfill the old covenant feast by his death and resurrection. What was about to occur would be the completion of that Passover.

Finally we read that they were gathered together in prayer (Acts 1:14). They did not go off to different locations, but they assembled to seek the Lord together. Like the Israelites on Sinai, they were prepared for what the Lord would do and were in fact together, *with one accord*, asking him with faith to do it.

The Event (The Experience)

When the day of Pentecost had come, they were all together in one place. And suddenly a sound came from heaven like the rush of a mighty wind, and it filled all the house where they were sitting. And there appeared to them tongues as of fire, distributed and resting on each one of them. And they were all filled with the Holy Spirit and began to speak in other tongues, as the Spirit gave them utterance. (Acts 2:1-4)

The second chapter of Acts begins with the description of the outpouring of the Spirit. While the first disciples were together, something striking happened to them. It had some notable similarities to what had happened on Sinai.

There was a sound like a mighty wind, a strong blowing sound. There was also, even more important, fire, the sign of God's presence when he appeared in the burning bush and in the pillar of fire. As we have seen, fire is a symbol for God. It is powerful enough to destroy. For those things ready to receive it, however, it can purify or refine. It can heat something up, giving a knife, for instance, the ability to burn or a pot the capacity to cook. It can unite things when, for instance, it bakes bread or fuses two pieces of metal together. Just as God descended in fire on Sinai to manifest himself to his people, so he descended on Mount Zion.

This time, however, God's descent was different. At Sinai he stood before them so that he might speak to them externally. On Mount Zion, however, the fire parted into separate flames, tongues of fire, and they were distributed and rested on each person present. These tongues represented the Holy Spirit, the fire of God's presence. All those who were part of the assembly were given a portion or share of the Holy Spirit. But since they were given a share in the Holy Spirit, they were given something that could not be divided up when it was distributed. In other words, they all shared in the same thing, the one fire of God. And that fire had not come just to stand before them and speak to them but to enter into them and change them and unite them.

The tongues of fire "rested on each." This was probably meant to signify that the Holy Spirit came to abide or remain in them, just as he had come to remain with Jesus (Jn 1:32). The coming of the Holy Spirit to the disciples was not just a transient phenomenon, as it was when the Spirit came upon the first elders of the people of Israel in Numbers 11 or upon a prophet so he could speak God's word or a judge so he could deliver God's people. It was to be an abiding presence within them.

The significance of the external sign of the tongues, distributed and resting upon the disciples, was summed up by the phrase "They were all filled with the Holy Spirit." In other words, the Holy Spirit entered into them to work in them. To this Luke adds, "And [they] began to speak in other tongues, as the Spirit gave them utterance." The presence of the Spirit in them had an external result. They began to speak—and to speak with words the Holy Spirit gave them. The interior experience was manifested in a way others could see. And it is not accidental that being filled with the Spirit and speaking in tongues were closely linked, as we shall see.

> Now there were dwelling in Jerusalem Jews, devout men from every nation under heaven. And at this sound the multitude came together, and they were bewildered, because each one heard them speaking in his own language. (Acts 2:5-6)

The first disciples, speaking together in tongues, attracted a crowd. The crowd was surprised by what they heard. The city was filled with Jews from the diaspora. Some of them perhaps had returned to live there, but many came for the feast, since this was the time of year when people could most safely and easily sail to the land of Israel across the Mediterranean. They were from all the known parts of the world, like pilgrims to Jerusalem today. And they could hear their own languages being spoken.

Luke probably did not narrate this part of the event just because it was miraculous but because it had great significance. To see that significance, we have to remember that God began to reverse the fall of the human race by choosing Abraham and working through him to create a people of his own. Just before the account of the call of Abraham, we can read about the Tower of Babel, the conclusion of the account of the fallen human race (Gn 4–11). The human beings in the account, the inhabitants of the most powerful civilized country of the day, decided, so to speak, to make use of their technology and form a corporate state that would run the whole human race. As the biblical account puts it, they decided to build "themselves" a city, in it to build a tower "with its top in the heavens," where they could rival God, and to make a name "for themselves." Their very success and impressiveness would keep them united.

God, however, came down, surveyed the situation, and decided that they had gone too far. He then scattered them by confusing their tongues so that they could not understand one another. Anyone who has taken an international flight on which the passengers cannot understand one another's languages will see how effective this can be in keeping people from interacting, much less working together.

On the Day of Pentecost, then, God came down again, but

this time to reverse what had happened at Babel. His goal was partly to restore his people, but he had in mind something greater: bringing back all the nations of the world so that they might be in relationship with him. His intention, in other words, was to complete his work with his old covenant people by empowering them so that their relationship with him could be opened to all the nations of the earth.

When God came down on the Day of Pentecost, then, he entered into the disciples of Christ so that he could make use of them. By filling the disciples, he could speak a message through each of them, a message described by one of the hearers as "telling in our own tongues [languages] the marvelous works of God." As a result the scattered people of the earth could hear the same truth and be brought to a relationship with God and so be united together because they would be united to him. For this reason, the Day of Pentecost has been referred to as the reversal of the Day of Babel.

> And all were amazed and perplexed, saying to one another, "What does this mean?" But others mocking said, "They are filled with new wine." (Acts 2:12-13)

One result of the outpouring of the Spirit on the disciples of Christ was confusion in those who witnessed it. Some were impressed. Others were dubious and mocked, saying that the disciples were drunk. This indicates something else to us. The first disciples must have had a strong experience, something that affected their behavior. In fact, they were "inebriated" but not with ordinary wine. They were inebriated with the Holy Spirit, the new wine that would renew God's people (see Mt 9:17 and parallels).

The Cause of the Event

But Peter, standing with the eleven, lifted up his voice and addressed them, "Men of Judea and all who dwell in Jerusalem, let this be known to you, and give ear to my words. For these men are not drunk, as you suppose, since it is only the third hour of the day; but this is what was spoken by the prophet Joel:

'And in the last days it shall be, God declares,
that I will pour out my Spirit upon all flesh,
and your sons and your daughters shall prophesy,
and your young men shall see visions,
and your old men shall dream dreams;
yea, and on my menservants and my maidservants in
    those days
I will pour out my Spirit; and they shall prophesy.
And I will show wonders in the heaven above
and signs on the earth beneath,
blood, and fire, and vapor of smoke;
the sun shall be turned into darkness
and the moon into blood,
before the day of the Lord comes,
the great and manifest day.
And it shall be that whoever calls on the name of the Lord
    shall be saved' [Joel 2:28-32]. (Acts 2:14-21)

Seeing the crowd gather and seeing their response, Peter stood up to explain what had happened. To do so, he preached the gospel of the death and resurrection of Christ for the first time. He began by quoting the prophecy of Joel that predicted the outpouring of the Holy Spirit upon all flesh. By all flesh the prophecy probably meant all sorts of people, not necessarily every individual.

The outpouring of the Spirit, according to Joel, was to happen before "the day of the Lord," what we have come to understand as the Day of Judgment. It would prepare people to go through the trials that would occur on that day. But not everyone will make it through that time of trial, because not everyone will have experienced the outpouring of the Holy Spirit and so be prepared. Only those who "call on the name of the Lord shall be saved." Peter then explained who *the Lord* is whom people need to call upon:

> Men of Israel, hear these words: Jesus of Nazareth, a man attested to you by God with mighty works and wonders and signs which God did through him in your midst, as you yourselves know—this Jesus, delivered up according to the definite plan and foreknowledge of God, you crucified and killed by the hands of lawless men....
>
> This Jesus God raised up, and of that we all are witnesses. Being therefore exalted at the right hand of God, and having received from the Father the promise of the Holy Spirit, he has poured out this which you see and hear....
>
> Let all the house of Israel therefore know assuredly that God has made him both Lord and Christ, this Jesus whom you crucified. (Acts 2:22-23, 32-33, 36)

The Lord who will save people on the Day of Judgment is Jesus of Nazareth. Those listening to Peter knew that Jesus had been crucified. Peter told them that he also rose and ascended to the right hand of the Father, there to share in the Father's reign over the earth. As a result of sharing God's throne, he received from his Father that which had been promised, the Holy Spirit, and he poured out that Spirit upon his apostles and those who were with them.

The cause of what had happened, of the experience that drew the crowd's attention, was the Lord himself. More precisely, it was the resurrection and ascension of the Lord, which put him in a position to pour out the Holy Spirit. The fulfillment of The Promise, then, came through the resurrection and ascension of Christ, events human beings could not see but which produced results in our world human beings could and still can see. It was those results that impressed the crowd.

They showed that Jesus was not just a condemned insurrectionist or blasphemer but the Lord and Christ. Only the Lord and Christ would be in the kind of relationship with the Father that meant he could pour out the Holy Spirit.

> Now when they heard this they were cut to the heart, and said to Peter and the rest of the apostles, "Brethren, what shall we do?" And Peter said to them, "Repent, and be baptized every one of you in the name of Jesus Christ for the forgiveness of your sins; and you shall receive the gift of the Holy Spirit. For the promise is to you and to your children and to all that are far off, every one whom the Lord our God calls to him." (Acts 2:37-39)

As a result of Peter's preaching, many of those who had heard him were "cut to the heart," affected in a way that meant they were ready to change. They desired to turn to the Lord. Peter then explained to them how they could do that. They needed to repent and be baptized, not with the baptism of John but in the name of Jesus Christ. As a result of that they too would receive the gift of the Holy Spirit. That gift was available not just to the original disciples but to every one whom the Lord calls to himself.

The Result

> So those who received his word were baptized, and there were added that day about three thousand souls. And they devoted themselves to the apostles' teaching and fellowship, to the breaking of bread and the prayers. And fear came upon every soul; and many wonders and signs were done through the apostles. (Acts 2:41-43)

Many accepted what Peter said and were baptized. Then it says, "There were added" three thousand people. They were added to a community, the body of believers in Christ, the Christian people, the first Christian church. A description of this community follows in Acts 2:42-47. A very similar description can be found in Acts 4:32-37.

The first item in the description of the first Christian community, *the apostles' teaching and fellowship [community]*, possibly refers to the common life created by the teaching about Christ and the new covenant in him, possibly to the regular gatherings with the apostles. *The breaking of bread* probably refers to what we would call the Lord's Supper or the Eucharist. *The prayers* is probably the regular daily and weekly prayers celebrated by the old covenant people, a pattern of prayer that was continued by believers in Christ. The grace of Pentecost, then, produced a renewal in worship of the Lord God.

The result was powerful witness, something that produced the fear of the Lord in others. This was reinforced by "many signs and wonders done through the apostles" because of the new power they had received through the outpouring of the Holy Spirit.

> And all who believed were together and had all things in common; and they sold their possessions and goods and distributed them to all, as any had need. (Acts 2:44-45)

The description continues by saying that all the believers were together and had all things in common. The early Christians did not scatter, filled with the Spirit and directed by him to go out into the entire world. The opposite happened. They came together and formed a community that was more united than human beings had been since the Tower of Babel or, more likely, since the Fall itself. Their oneness was a sign of the Spirit's being in them.

They were *together*. Even though, as is clear from the description of the first Christians in the early chapters of Acts, they all did not live in one building or on one plot of ground, they came together regularly and shared their lives in various ways. They also had "all things in common." This probably did not mean that they had the equivalent of one bank account, a system of common finances, but that they recognized the claim that their brothers and sisters in Christ had upon their personal finances and so were willing to share what they had when others had need. The first Christians had become "spiritual" in a new way, and this was not just expressed in direct relationship with God but also in relationship with one another. The grace of Pentecost, then, produced a renewal in community, what we might speak of as Christian community.

> And day by day, attending the temple together and breaking bread in their homes, they partook of food with glad and generous hearts, praising God and having favor with all the people. And the Lord added to their number day by day those who were being saved. (Acts 2:46-47)

The new life of the first believers was expressed partly in sharing in the temple prayers and partly in eucharistic gatherings among themselves. They were visible enough to those around them, and their spiritual commitment was obvious enough, that their life had an impact on others. No doubt there was individual evangelism, but the account in Acts 2 emphasizes that it was their life together that impacted others. The result of the outpouring of the Holy Spirit was a community living "in the Spirit," and this drew others to the Lord. The grace of Pentecost, then, produced effective evangelism.

The New Covenant Blessing

The fulness of the new covenant blessing, "the fulness of the blessing of Christ" (Rom 15:29), was given on Pentecost. Pentecost is the day that the risen Lord baptized the first group of his disciples in the Spirit. What he gave then is the grace of Pentecost, a grace intended to produce a certain kind of life. It is this that we are seeking to live.

We have experienced in recent years a renewal of the grace of Pentecost among Christian people. Some of those who have entered into this renewal were Jews or pagans. Like those present on the first Day of Pentecost or at subsequent outpourings of the Holy Spirit described in the Acts of the Apostles, they were not Christians at all. For them, becoming a Christian and receiving the gift of the Holy Spirit or the grace of Pentecost were all the same event.

Others who have entered into this renewal had been Christians for many years. Some were barely Christians, acknowledging the name on census forms but not having much more Christianity than that. Others have been church attendees, regular in some level of Christian life but deficient in others. Others have been committed Christians, believing the creed, keeping the commandments, and being active in a church or some Christian group. Yet they all would say that they received the grace of Pentecost as a result of turning to the Lord, perhaps in a program like the Life in the Spirit Seminars, perhaps in some prayer session, perhaps some other way.

Few of them, of course, would speak about receiving the grace of Pentecost in those words. They would say that they had an experience that changed their Christian life. They would call that experience an experience of the Holy Spirit's working in them in a new way, one that gave them an experiential relationship with Christ. It would not be uncommon for them to simply say that before they did not know the Lord and now they do.

This new experience has been spoken about in varying ways. The most common way is to speak of "the baptism in the Spirit" or "being baptized in the Spirit." In other languages, it is more common to speak of "the outpouring of the Holy Spirit." Some, mainly denominational Pentecostals, will speak of "receiving the Holy Spirit."

There are many theological views of what happens to people when they are baptized in the Spirit. This book is not about baptism in the Spirit. (For a treatment of the most important questions about this, see "Understanding Baptism in the Holy Spirit" in my book *Baptized in the Holy Spirit,* reprinted by Tabor House, 2004.) It is, however, important to understand, for what follows in this book, that most people, when they are baptized in the Spirit, are not simply receiving the Spirit for the first time. Rather something new happens to them in relationship to the Holy Spirit.

All Christians have the Holy Spirit; otherwise they are not Christians. Paul says in Romans 8:9 that "any one who does not have the Spirit of Christ does not belong to him." Unless we want to deny that all those who have not been baptized in the Spirit are Christians, we have to accept the fact that many of them had the Holy Spirit before in some sense.

On the other hand, for most of them something was obviously missing. They came to recognize that their experience of the Christian life was not the same as what was described in the Acts of the Apostles or even in the experience of many other Christians today. They may have believed the truths, kept the commandments, and attended church, but the experiential aspect was either missing or attenuated. They were much like the disciples before Pentecost. They related to Christ but in a somewhat old covenant way. They related to God, as did the Jews on Mount Sinai, as someone outside themselves, helping them, but not someone they could experience directly and at work inside themselves. When they were baptized in the Spirit, that changed.

To explain how the Holy Spirit can be in someone without having much effect, the example of a sound system is sometimes used. When a sound system is brought into a room for the first time, it is inert. It is a mechanism that cannot do anything. When it is plugged in, it then has electricity in it. But it is still not capable of amplifying sound. It also has to be switched on. When someone is baptized in the Spirit, the presence of the Holy Spirit is "switched on." It is not that he was not there at all, but now his presence and the results of his presence can be experienced.

Another example that is sometimes used is that of a piece of frozen meat. When it is taken out of the freezer, it may be a perfectly good piece of meat, but it cannot be eaten. It has to be put on a grill or stove. When fire (heat) is passed through it, a change occurs, and then it can be eaten. Nothing new has been added to the frozen meat, but as a result of being heated, now it tastes good and can be eaten. The Christian life of many was like that frozen piece of meat before they were baptized in the Spirit. It was all there, but it was not as much good to them as it was supposed to be.

We use the word *renewal* to speak of what happens to people as a result of being baptized in the Spirit. We describe it as a renewal in the church or a renewal of the church or of its life. *Renewal* indicates for us that people are not finding something that had been completely missing, but that something already there in some way is becoming effective. It is a real change, not just a realization of what we already had but a renewal of the presence in us of the Spirit, who already had been given to us.

The renewal in the Spirit, however, is not intended to be a one-time experience. It is not intended to simply let us know that the Lord is real and then let our lives go back to what they were before. It is intended to be a renewal of the grace of Pentecost, a grace that is supposed to remain in us.

Pentecost occurred because the Lord had a purpose in redeeming us. The Holy Spirit was poured out not just so that our sins could be forgiven, although they needed to be forgiven for us to receive the outpouring. The Spirit was poured out—on the Day of Pentecost on Mount Zion almost two thousand years ago—so that the purpose of Pentecost on Mount Sinai could be accomplished effectively—so that there could be a redeemed people in covenant relationship with God, a people who love God and love their neighbor.

The gift of the Spirit makes a change so that Christians should not be just a people who read the Law, the expression of God's will, and then try to live it on their own. As Paul put it in 2 Corinthians 3:3, new covenant people who have received the gift of the Spirit should be "a letter from Christ delivered by us [to be known and read by all men], written not with ink but with the Spirit of the living God, not on tablets of stone but on tablets of human hearts [literally, hearts of flesh]." A body of Christians should be a people in whom the prophecy of Ezekiel has been fulfilled. The law should be written inside of them and should change the way they live. As a result, others should be able to "know and read" their lives and come to know the truth of the gospel.

We have "a new covenant, not in a written code but in the Spirit; for the written code kills, but the Spirit gives life" (2 Cor 3:6). In this book we are not interested in the initial experience of the Holy Spirit and how the Holy Spirit is given but in the result: having the new covenant life inside of us with love of God and neighbor written upon our hearts by the Spirit. We are interested in the ongoing life of the Spirit and how to live it in a daily way. For that we need what we have been calling a charismatic spirituality.

THIS GIVES US OUR FIRST CONCLUSION:

Charismatic spirituality is based on the understanding that the gift of the Holy Spirit is the specific newness of the new covenant (the gift or grace Christ came to bring), and we should experience this gift as the basis of a new relationship with God.

CHAPTER TWO

Being Spiritual

One of my earliest memories comes from a time when I was working with my father. He used to have me help him when he worked around the house. Because I was so young that I could hardly do anything, he had me bring him things. In doing that I learned what tools were and what they were for.

One day he was repairing a washing machine, and he asked me to get him the screwdriver. I did not know what he wanted until he pointed to it. I then realized that he wanted what I had thought was a paint can opener. At that point I came into a new understanding of screwdrivers. Their purpose, what they had been created for, was not to open paint cans but to turn screws. If I had never understood that, I would never have been able to screw and unscrew things. Other things can be used to open paint cans, but it takes a screwdriver to turn screws.

Now, there is nothing wrong with using a screwdriver to open paint cans. A screwdriver makes an excellent paint can opener. But if I had never learned what screwdrivers were made for, I would not be able to do many things in life that I now can.

Something similar is true for what we have come to call the baptism in the Spirit. In recent years in the charismatic renewal movement, various things have come to the fore. For a period of time it was healing. You could have thought that charismatic renewal was a healing movement. Another focus has been spiritual gifts. It is now very common to hear people explain the charismatic renewal as a movement for the restoration of spiritual gifts. Equally strong has been spiritual experiences. Many sound as if they think that the key to good spiritual life is to be "slain in the Spirit" and to have some spiritual experience in the process.

Now, none of these things is unconnected with baptism in the Spirit. It is the gateway to healing (or to praying for others for healing). It does lead to spiritual gifts, as well as to spiritual experiences. But if we ask the question, what is baptism in the Spirit for? Or, what is the grace of Pentecost for? None of those is an adequate answer. The Spirit was not given on the Day of Pentecost so that we could be healed or have spiritual gifts or have spiritual experiences. It was given so that God could have a people who were in effective covenant relationship with him, who loved him and loved one another because the law was written on their hearts and because they had been given life and power through the Holy Spirit to do so.

In the last chapter we looked at the outpouring of the Spirit in God's plan. We sought to understand why God decided to give his Spirit to human beings, what that action of his was supposed to bring about. Now we will look at its purpose in our own lives. We will ask the question, What is the gift of the Holy Spirit supposed to do for us as individuals?

Being Spiritual People

In the third chapter of 1 Corinthians, there is a passage that provides a fundamental insight into the work of the Spirit in us (vv. 1-4). Paul was speaking to the Corinthians, a church he had founded, and said:

> But I, brethren, could not address you as spiritual men, but as men of the flesh, as babes in Christ. I fed you with milk, not solid food; for you were not ready for it; and even yet you are not ready, for you are still of the flesh. For while there is jealousy and strife among you, are you not of the flesh, and behaving like ordinary men? For when one says, "I belong to Paul," and another, "I belong to Apollos," are you not merely men?

There were a number of problems in the newly established Christian community at Corinth when Paul wrote this letter. The chief seemed to have been serious disunity resulting in factionalization, which was threatening to lead to division. As we can see in the above passage, Paul attributed this to the fact that the Corinthians were not spiritual people. They were, as he put it, "of the flesh" and "behaving like ordinary human beings," rather than like Christians.

To understand what he meant by that, it is helpful to look at what he said to them in the first chapter of 1 Corinthians in verses 4-11:

> I give thanks to God always for you because of the grace of God which was given you in Christ Jesus, that in every way you were enriched in him with all speech and all knowledge—even as the testimony to Christ was confirmed among you—so that you are not lacking in any spiritual gift, as you wait for the revealing of our Lord Jesus Christ; who will sustain you to the end, guiltless in the day of our Lord Jesus Christ. God is faithful, by whom you were called into the fellowship of his Son, Jesus Christ our Lord.
>
> I appeal to you, brethren, by the name of our Lord Jesus Christ, that all of you agree and that there be no dissensions among you, but that you be united in the same mind and the same judgment. For it has been reported to me by Chloe's people that there is quarreling among you, my brethren.

At the outset of the letter the lack of unity in the Corinthian church was clearly on Paul's mind. There were dissensions and quarreling. Nonetheless he began by thanking God for them because they had received the grace of God. Even more, he said that they had received all the spiritual gifts. Now, here is something extraordinary. The Corinthians had been baptized in the Spirit and had all the spiritual gifts, but as Paul said in Chapter 3, they were not spiritual!

To understand what Paul is saying, we first need to understand that when *spiritual* is used in the New Testament, it almost never means "immaterial." Rather, it means "of" or "related to" the Holy Spirit. Something is spiritual when it comes from the Holy Spirit or is somehow connected to the Holy Spirit. Second, we can usefully retranslate the word *spiritual* as "spiritualized." This will allow us to speak and think more clearly about what Paul is saying.

As we can see from comparing the above two passages, the fact that the Corinthians were not spiritual did not mean that they were without the gift of the Holy Spirit. Nor did it mean that they had not experienced the Holy Spirit at work in and through them (see 1:4; Rom 8:9). Rather, it means that the presence of the Spirit in them had not transformed them, at least not in one very important respect. In short, there is a difference between having the Spirit present in us, even working through us, and being spiritual people, or more clearly put, being spiritualized people.

Being "of the flesh," as used in 1 Corinthians 3:1, means behaving in a way that is not spiritual. *Flesh* in this context refers to unredeemed human nature, so those who are "of the flesh" relate in a way that is characteristic of unredeemed people. They are like ordinary people, that is, people who have never been spiritualized.

Jealousy and strife were the signs that something was seriously wrong. The phrase "among you" indicates that the problem was corporate (and therefore that the problem was not necessarily with all the members). In other words, the

Corinthian community was acting in a way that indicated it had not been fully spiritualized, and this was manifested in the way many of the members related to one another.

Not all conflict is seriously wrong, but if it turns into hostility or disunity (factionalizing) within a body of Christians, something is wrong. Of course, the cause of the problem might only be some people who are not spiritualized—it only takes one side to start a war—but the existence of the war at least indicates something seriously wrong. Paul, then, was probably talking about a community problem and indicating that it was due to the fact that members of the community, some at least, were not yet spiritualized in how they related to the life of the community and to one another. In short, the sign of deficient spiritualization in this instance was a personal relationship problem, a problem in love of neighbor.

In order to see the positive side, to see what spiritualization should look like when it is present, we will look at a different passage; sometimes referred to as the Fruit of the Spirit Passage:

> For you were called to freedom, brethren; only do not use your freedom as an opportunity for the flesh, but through love be servants of one another. For the whole law is fulfilled in one word, "You shall love your neighbor as yourself" [Lv 19:18]. But if you bite and devour one another take heed that you are not consumed by one another. But I say, walk by the Spirit, and do not gratify the desires of the flesh....
>
> Now the works of the flesh are plain: immorality, impurity, licentiousness, idolatry, sorcery, enmity, strife, jealousy, anger, selfishness, dissension, party spirit, envy, drunkenness, carousing, and the like. I warn you, as I warned you before, that those who do such things shall not inherit the kingdom of God. But the fruit of the Spirit is love, joy, peace, patience, kindness, goodness, faithfulness, gentleness, self-control; against such there is no law. And those who belong to Christ Jesus have crucified the flesh with its passions and desires.

> If we live by the Spirit, let us also walk by the Spirit. Let us
> have no self-conceit, no provoking of one another, no envy of
> one another. (Galatians 5:13-16, 19-26)

To understand this passage, we should recall some background. Galatians was written in response to people sometimes referred to as Judaizers, who wanted all Christians to "live like Jews" (2:14), especially to be circumcised and keep the law of Moses. This implied that Christians who had been pagans (Gentiles) needed initiation into the old covenant in order to receive the full benefit of Christianity. Paul rejected such a view.

In the course of the letter, Paul taught that being in Christ and having received the Holy Spirit included all that the old covenant provided and more. It was therefore unnecessary for Christians to add old covenant practices, like circumcision, to new covenant life. These practices did not effect a better or fuller relationship with God, and to say that they did was to deny an essential truth about what Christ did for us. On the other hand, Paul had to rule out the misconception that we could be in Christ and live any way we want just because we have been freed from the old covenant law, and so we have the exhortation in Chapter 5 on the fruit of the Spirit.

Paul began by saying that the Galatian Christians were "called to freedom," probably meaning freedom from those aspects of the old covenant approach that came from its purpose in dealing with human sinfulness and imperfection. But he insisted that this freedom was not just lack of restraint. God did not free us so there would be "an opportunity for the flesh," that is, so that the flesh, our unredeemed nature, could have its way unrestrained. Rather he intended us to serve one another in love. Christian freedom is the freedom to be what we were meant to be—sons and daughters of God and therefore people who live in his image and likeness.

In the course of the passage, Paul listed "works of the

flesh." These are the things the flesh will work [do] if left to it-self. They include fornication, sexual impurity, idolatry, enmity, strife, and so on. We would normally call these sins. They are patterns of behavior that are forbidden by God.

Instead of "gratifying the desires of the flesh," that is, al-lowing the flesh to do what it wants, we need to "walk by the Spirit." *Walking* is a Hebrew idiom for "behaving," that is, for living a certain way. The way we walk is the way we live. This new way we should live will naturally tend to grow when the Holy Spirit is in us; thus we call it the fruit of the Spirit. The list of the fruit of the Spirit includes love, joy, peace, patience, kind-ness, and the like. The fruit that the Spirit produces, then, is good patterns of behavior or character traits, good ways of treat-ing others, good ways of handling the circumstances of life.

There is an intrinsic connection between the Holy Spirit and the fruit of the Spirit. The Holy Spirit is the Spirit of God, and God has certain characteristics. He is loving, joyful, peace-ful, patient, kind, and so on. So the presence of God's Spirit in us tends to make us act the way he himself would. The Scriptures also talk about the result as our being formed in the image and likeness of God (see, for instance, Col 3:10 and 2 Cor 3:18). If the Holy Spirit is in us, he will be about restoring the image and likeness of God in us, making us more like God in the way we live.

This truth is sometimes expressed in a different terminol-ogy. Christian teachers, especially those who lived in Western (Latin) Europe during the Middle Ages and later teachers who have been influenced by them, sometimes speak about infused virtues. By virtues they mean good character traits or good pat-terns of behavior. When they say these virtues are infused, they mean that the Holy Spirit, who has filled us, produces these virtues in us (pours them into us, so to speak). They are not just acquired by our own efforts but are given to us by the work of the Holy Spirit. The term "infused virtue," then, is another way of speaking about the fruit of the Spirit.

Paul concluded with an important distinction when he said that if we live by the Spirit, we should also walk by the Spirit, or translated differently, if we have life from the Spirit, we should also live in a spiritualized way. In Romans 8, a similar passage, Paul makes the same distinction by speaking of "the Spirit of God [who] dwells in you" (8:9, 11) and "gives [you] life" (8:10-11) and of our walking (8:4) or living according to the Spirit (8:5). In other words, Christ's gift of the Spirit—that is, his gift of new life through the Spirit—does not guarantee that we will turn out the way he intended when he gave us the gift. We will not necessarily become spiritualized and so live in a spiritual way. It is one thing to live by the Spirit or have new life through the Spirit. It is another thing to walk in the Spirit, that is, to live in a spiritualized way.

The description Paul gave of what the gift of the Spirit should produce makes the results sound automatic, as if once we have received the Spirit, all we need to do is put up our feet, lay back, and let good character and excellent behavior just grow—no fuss, no muss, and no effort. Now, Paul certainly meant to convey the fact there is a new spiritual life put inside of us that gives us a new capacity and desire to live the way God wants us to. He did not, however, intend to convey that we will end up living that life automatically, with no effort.

The way Paul exhorted the Galatians to show the fruit of the Spirit makes clear that there is a matter of choice and effort on our part. We have to "crucify the flesh," put the flesh to death—that is, deliberately choose to depart from the old way of life. We also have to continue to avoid the old way of life. We have to, in an ongoing way, refuse to follow the flesh, the unredeemed or untransformed tendencies that are still within in us. As Paul said in a similar passage (Rom 8:13), "If by the Spirit you put to death the deeds of the body, you will live." We can successfully choose to live differently, but we need to be resolute about doing so. We can do that by the power the Spirit gives us.

If we need to choose to live in the new way, we need a criterion to judge when we are being spiritual or not. This is why the word of God—Scripture and Christian teaching—is so important. We cannot always determine what is spiritual by direct intuition or discernment. We need to know what God intends the gift of his Spirit to produce in us so that we are not led astray (1 Cor 12:2) or deceived (1 Jn 2:26). We need to be able to test the Spirits (1 Jn 4:4) and so need to know the signs of the work of the Holy Spirit.

The criterion Paul gave us in the passages we have been reading are keeping the commandments, which means turning away from the works of the flesh and exhibiting the fruit of the Spirit in the way we relate to others. We do not need to do extraordinary things to be spiritual. We do not have to perform miracles or have great spiritual experiences as Paul did (see 2 Cor 12:1-4). But we do need to treat others, our brothers and sisters in Christ, well. The sign of being spiritual, then, is loving God and neighbor (v. 14).

The well-known passage in 1 Corinthians 13:1-7, the "love passage," is in fact about the importance of the right criterion to evaluate our spiritual condition:

> If I speak in the tongues of men and of angels, but have not love, I am a noisy gong or a clanging cymbal. And if I have prophetic powers, and understand all mysteries and all knowledge, and if I have all faith, so as to remove mountains, but have not love, I am nothing. If I give away all I have, and if I deliver my body to be burned, but have not love, I gain nothing.
>
> Love is patient and kind; love is not jealous or boastful; it is not arrogant or rude. Love does not insist on its own way; it is

> not irritable or resentful; it does not rejoice at wrong, but rejoices in the right. Love bears all things, believes all things, hopes all things, endures all things.

Paul was not saying that speaking in tongues, prophesying, understanding mysteries, moving mountains, giving away all our possessions, and letting ourselves be killed in martyrdom are bad without love. He was, however, saying that those things are not criteria of whether we are doing well. That criterion is love, the fruit of the Spirit. The presence or absence of the fruit of the Spirit in our lives will tell us if we are spiritualized people or not.

The communitarian aspect of being spiritualized also needs to be emphasized, because we live in such an individualistic culture that we tend to interpret the above passages as simply being about individual Christians. We easily overlook the fact that Paul was trying to instruct a group of Christians about how to live together, about how to be a body of people filled with the one Spirit of God. Even as individuals, we can only successfully become a dwelling place of God in the Spirit by being built into the new temple—the Christian people, the church—as we can see in Ephesians 2:17-22:

> And he came and preached peace to you who were far off and peace to those who were near; for through him we both have access in one Spirit to the Father. So then you are no longer strangers and sojourners, but you are fellow citizens with the saints and members of the household of God, built upon the foundation of the apostles and prophets, Christ Jesus himself being the cornerstone, in whom the whole structure is joined together and grows into a holy temple in the Lord; in whom you also are built into it for a dwelling place of God in the Spirit.

There is, then, a direct connection between being built into a body of Christians and living the life of the Spirit. We normally do not come first to life spiritually and then unite ourselves to others who are also alive spiritually. Rather, it is as we are joined to a body of Christians that the Holy Spirit comes to dwell in us in an ongoing way. We receive help to live the life of the Spirit by being part of a community that is living the life of the Spirit.

Two truths are linked here and elsewhere in Scripture. On the one hand, we become spiritual or spiritualized by living in a body of people who are living the life of the Spirit. On the other hand, relating to one another in a good way makes us a fitting place for the Holy Spirit to dwell. Relating to other Christians in a good way should increase spiritual life in us, just as letting the Holy Spirit dwell in us should bear fruit in relating well to others. True spiritual life and Christian community go together.

The chief criterion, then, of being spiritual is how we love one another in a daily life way. Good relationships among Christians is what makes a body of Christians a truly spiritual temple. We are filled with the Spirit so that we can be a temple to the glory of God, a body of people who love God and love one another.

An Experiential Relationship With God

The gift of the Spirit gives us power to live the Christian life, to walk in the Spirit, in part by making our relationship with God experiential. The experiential aspect is only one component of good Christian living. We also need orthodox beliefs. We need practical wisdom for how to deal with the various things we come across in life. We need to repent of our sin, and so on. In speaking about the experiential aspect of our Christian life, we are only focusing on one feature of Christian life. Nonetheless, it is an important one.

For many, Christianity is a matter of ideas, either about what happened in the past (the events narrated in Scripture) or about doctrine and morality. They think they mainly need to "live up to" what they have been taught. Relationship with God in Christ, however, should not be just a matter of ideas, however true we believe them to be or however well we try to live up to them. It should be something experienced in our world, experienced as real (objective) and personal, a relationship with a person with whom we interact. We can, in other words, make contact with God and know that we have done so. To use the word we will use for such objective, interactive contact with God: We can and should *experience* him and his presence with us. To use the scriptural phrase: We can "know the Lord" (Jer 31:34).

We can see in a number of passages in Scripture that experience is an integral part of the Christian life. The most striking one is Galatians 3:1-5:

> O foolish Galatians! Who has bewitched you, before whose eyes Jesus Christ was publicly portrayed as crucified? Let me ask you only this: Did you receive the Spirit by works of the law, or by hearing with faith? Are you so foolish? Having begun with the Spirit, are you now ending with the flesh? Did you experience so many things in vain?—if it really is in vain. Does he who supplies the Spirit to you and works miracles among you do so by works of the law, or by hearing with faith?

In this passage Paul shows that he expected all the Christians in the Galatian church to have had an experiential relationship with God. He asked two linked questions: Did you experience so many things in vain? and Does he who supplies the Spirit to you and works miracles among you do so by works of the law, or by hearing with faith? The striking thing is that he actually expected them to be able to answer the questions; otherwise he would not have made his point. He expected them to know, from experience, how they received the Spirit and how they, or at least some of them, worked miracles.

The answer to Paul's rhetorical questions, of course, is that the Galatian Christians experienced the gift of the Spirit by hearing with faith, not by being circumcised and following the ceremony of the old covenant law. We will consider the importance of hearing with faith in the next two chapters. Here it is enough for us to see that Paul actually expected the Christians he had raised up to have experienced the Spirit and spiritual gifts.

Such a view is not restricted to Paul. The First Letter of John says the same thing in an equally explicit way, in verse 4:13: "By this we know that we abide in him and he in us, because he has given us of his own Spirit." Verse 3:24 says something similar: "All who keep his commandments abide in him, and he in them. And by this we know that he abides in us, by the Spirit which he has given us."

The First Letter of John was written to help a group of early Christians judge whether they were true Christians, truly spiritual people, or not. This had become important because they needed to be able to distinguish between Christian spirituality and that of certain people, sometimes called Proto-Gnostics, who claimed to be the truly spiritual ones. According to 1 John, the criteria of true (Christian) spirituality are whether people believe in the incarnation of Christ, whether they keep the commandments, and whether they love other Christians—as well as whether they have experienced the Spirit. In the above two passages, then, John was saying that Christians should know that they have a true relationship with Christ—that is, that they abide in him and he in them—by their experience of the Spirit.

The above set of passages tells us that Christians should experience the Spirit, and others could be added. If we cannot point our finger to anything definite in our experience that indicates the presence of the Spirit, the questions or comments in these passages make no sense. If that is the case, then our Christian life is missing something. We should have an experience of Christ as a real person, an existent being who is something other than us (and not just an aspect of us, our "spiritual selves," as New Age people sometimes say). And we should have an experience of the Spirit Christ has given us, present in us and working through us.

Although the truth about the experiential nature of Christianity is important, it has to be approached with some caution. Our goal should not be to have spiritual experiences but to have a good relationship with God that is experiential. We do not want to become "experience-focused."

We live in a time when a large number of people are focused on experience. They are especially seeking experiences with high subjective interest, excitement, personal satisfaction. We can see this in many ways. About fifteen years or so ago, I came across a striking example in an article. The writer had noticed a new phenomenon: The first feminists were starting to have babies. Since the early feminist movement was most noted for women's advancement in the workplace and outside the home, this new interest in babies was newsworthy.

The article contained interviews of women who had recently had babies and were answering the question of why they had them. One of those interviewed expressed a common opinion: "I knew I was getting older and soon would not be able to have a baby. I did not want to miss the experience of having a baby, so I had one."

That is an extraordinary approach to having a baby. She did not have a baby because the baby was important to her, because a new living human being would come into the world. She wanted to have a baby so she could have an experience! It would be hard to find a better example of how experience-focused our age can be, and yet many of us do not even notice such things because they are so common.

Such an orientation is all around us. New Age religion is

very experience-focused. To many proponents of New Age teaching, it does not seem important what god or spirit or spiritual force they might be experiencing. The important thing is that they are experiencing something spiritual. And they do not seem to be at all concerned that there might be any bad effects from experiencing a relationship with an evil spirit.

Christians too can be experience-focused. Charismatics can be especially prone to this, seeking leadings, times of "slaying" or "resting" in the Spirit, "divine appointments," on so on. Such things become a center of attention, even the goal of the Christian life, rather than a spiritual help in the course of seeking a good relationship with the Lord. This too is probably a result of the times we are living in.

To understand what it means to say our relationship with the Lord should be experiential and why spiritual experience is important, we need to clear away some misconceptions about experience. First, human experience is not always exciting, stimulating, emotionally moving. We might touch a live electric wire. That would be an exciting, stimulating and moving experience. But we also might watch a boring movie. We would still be having an experience, even if we were uninterested and unmoved, at least up to the point when we might fall asleep.

Knowing that we can have human experience without excitement or much subjective stimulation has special relevance to our understanding of our spiritual life. We often have to live through periods when we cannot experience much in a lively way, and yet those are often times when we most need to relate to the Lord. The way we experience life changes when we get sick, for instance. We are usually dulled in our ability to respond to and appreciate things. If at such a time we evaluate our prayer life, for example, by how much we are moved by it or how immediately interested we are in praying, we might be tempted to give up praying at a time when we most need to pray.

Something similar is true of old age. As we get older, we do not respond as immediately to people and events as when we were younger. If we have to be excited, stimulated, and moved in order to believe that we are having significant experiences, we will be tempted to evaluate our experience of personal relationships and relationship with God as getting poorer as we get older, when instead it is just changing with age and may even be getting deeper in many respects.

Not only is experience not always exciting, stimulating, and moving; it is often not conscious or adverted to, surprising as that seems to many. In fact, we very commonly do not notice what we are experiencing. There is an experience that you are having right now but almost certainly are not noticing: You are breathing. Now that I have mentioned it, you are conscious of it. Moreover, you know that two minutes ago or ten minutes ago you were having the same experience, but you had not adverted to it.

We most often notice or are conscious of our experiences when there is a change, when something new happens. If we stop breathing, we very quickly have a conscious experience of our breathing or, to be more precise, of the fact that our breathing has ceased. Or if we smell something pleasant and make a point of inhaling to get more of the fragrance, we likely will notice our breathing. We also become conscious of our experiences when there is some difficulty related to them. People with asthma or some other breathing difficulty are often more regularly conscious of their breathing.

The same thing is true of our personal relationships. I recently went to a funeral of an old acquaintance. At the funeral

I noticed that one of my friends was crying during the service. This surprised me because I had not thought he had had that much of a relationship with the dead man, so I asked him about it. He responded that he was surprised, too. He said, "I had not realized how important he was to me until he was gone and I missed him." Very often that is the case. We only realize the depth or strength of relationships with people we live with or see regularly when those relationships are lost or are threatened.

Though experience does not always have a high immediate impact, nonetheless the presence or absence of an experience of something, especially of a personal relationship with someone, is important. It changes our lives in objective ways, some big, some small.

One of the members of our community comes from Fiji. He studied in England, became part of the university outreach there, and then stayed to be part of the community. I knew him for many years, and I knew that he had a father who was still alive because he talked about him. But his father was always in Fiji or at least some place other than where I was. I had a certain relationship with the father in that we knew of one another and both knew that we had a relationship with his son.

One day I happened to be in London when the father, who worked in the Fijian diplomatic service, came on a mission. We had lunch with him right after he arrived on a plane from Fiji, and that was my chance to meet him. Now, I have a great deal of sympathy for people just getting off a plane from a long flight and trying to cope with a new time zone and country, because I do that frequently and can feel a bit like a zombie. My friend's father is always gracious, and the lunch was pleasant enough, but he was clearly tired and much less lively than usual. Having lunch with him was not an exciting, stimulating, moving experience.

Nonetheless it was an important event: I made his acquaintance personally. Before I had known about him; now I knew him—experientially. That changed our relationship, establishing it in a personal way. Since then I have gone to Fiji. Because I knew him, I stayed at his house. In the course of being there he told me many things about Fiji, Fijian society, and Fijian history that most Americans would never know. Once when he was a Fijian senator, I was able to go to a meeting of the national senate. Many things happened differently thereafter because I had had an objective experience, the simple objective experience of meeting him.

The same thing is true of our relationship with God. There is a big difference between knowing about God and knowing him from experience. Experiential knowledge of God allows us to enter into a relationship with him that is personal and more dynamic than it would be otherwise. That is the case whether we experience it as exciting or routine, whether we consciously advert to it or take it for granted.

We can lead a good Christian life without having made experiential contact with the Lord. Many have, but it is more difficult, because the experiential aspect of the relationship with God imparts vitality and strength. That is why many people after they have been baptized in the Spirit get a "spiritual high." They have experienced a major change for the better in their Christian life, and they notice it at once.

For others, an experiential relationship with the Lord comes about more gradually, like slowly developing a friendship with someone we live with for many years. Nonetheless, it still makes their Christian life more vital, even though they cannot date the beginning of a change.

It is also true that our experience of Christian life, our experience of God, is often ordinary, even routine, like most of our experience of life. If we evaluate our Christian experience by how we consciously feel about it, or even more, by how exciting, stimulating, or moving it is, we might be tempted to think that "God has gone away," or we "lost it," or "it faded away." That could be the case. Some people have lost their relationship with God or it has become weak. But it is rarely the case that people are concerned about their relationship with God when they do not have much of one. They are usually concerned because they do have a significant relationship with God, but something has changed in the way they experience it.

The question, then, is how can we evaluate our spiritual experience. We can find the answer in many parts of the New Testament. A short statement of it can be found in Colossians 1:9-13:

> And so, from the day we heard of it, we have not ceased to pray for you, asking that you may be filled with the knowledge of his will in all spiritual wisdom and understanding, to lead a life worthy of the Lord, fully pleasing to him, bearing fruit in every good work and increasing in the knowledge of God. May you be strengthened with all power, according to his glorious might, for all endurance and patience with joy, giving thanks to the Father, who has qualified us to share in the inheritance of the saints in light. He has delivered us from the dominion of darkness and transferred us to the kingdom of his beloved Son.

Paul in this passage gives a sketch of how spiritual experience should function. First of all, it is not an end in itself. The true end or goal of the Christian life is "to lead a life worthy of the Lord, fully pleasing to him, bearing fruit in every good work, and increasing in the knowledge of God." The goal, in other words, is love of God and love of neighbor. To make this possible, the Holy Spirit works inside of us, equipping us to live the way God wants us to. Our experience of the work of the Holy Spirit, then, should be manifested in how we do God's will, and therefore doing God's will is the main criterion for evaluating our spiritual experience.

In saying this, the above passage contains much the same point as the passages we looked at in the first part of this chapter, but it adds a couple important truths that help us to recognize when the Holy Spirit has been active. First, it makes clear that one of the ways the Holy Spirit works in us is to give us "spiritual wisdom and understanding." He provides light for our minds so that we can know God and know his will. Second, it makes clear that he also strengthens us interiorly so that we can go through trials and sufferings in a good way. The fact that he gives us light and strength is noteworthy, partly because many Christians tend to assume that the only way to discern the working of the Holy Spirit in us is by feeling him move inside or perhaps by feeling a desire to do something.

To say that the Holy Spirit gives us light does not mean that every time he does so we have a conscious experience of being enlightened, although that often happens. Nor does it mean that whenever the Holy Spirit strengthens us, we have a conscious experience of being strengthened, though that, too, happens. More commonly, our experience is of having new spiritual wisdom and understanding or having greater strength, at the same time knowing that we did not produce these things ourselves but seem to have received them in our relationship with God. The way to evaluate what is happening with us spiritually is by considering how well we are able to live our Christian life as a whole, not how often we have a strong conscious awareness of the Spirit working in us, much less how often we "feel" him at work in us.

Our conscious experiences of the Holy Spirit are only intended to equip us to live a life pleasing to God, and if they do not do that, they are not benefiting us and may be merely emotional and not genuinely spiritual. We might, for instance, go to a charismatic conference or prayer meeting and have a very good experience. We might be "in the heavenlies" and leave that meeting enthused and uplifted. Then we might get up the next morning and come down to the breakfast table. We find our wife a little grumpier than usual. We find ourselves more irritable than normal because of the late return we had the night before. Our young son spills the milk all over us. Even worse, he spills it on the last clean shirt we have. We finally get to the car and drive away late. On the way it seems as if every light we come to is red. When we get to work, we remember that we were supposed to meet with our boss the first thing in the morning and now he is waiting for us. At that point the question is, What good was going to the prayer meeting and being in the heavenlies?

The answer should be that it is good if it helps us to make a good response to our boss, to our family, to our daily life responsibilities. If we handle better our relationships with our wife and children, with our job—and with the Lord himself—at least over time, then it has been good. If not, it has been not good or it has been, at best, neutral. We need to be spiritual at home and at work, not just at the prayer meeting or in conferences. If we have a job, are married, have a family to raise, that is where our vocation is. Our spiritual experiences at the prayer meeting or conference should help us to love God and love our neighbor in our daily life, to live our vocation well. If so, they have helped us to be spiritualized people. Christian spiritual experience should equip us to live daily life better, the daily life we are called to.

It should also help us to live Christian life for the long haul. Much of life is routine and should be. We cannot constantly live in a state of excitement or constantly have everything new and interesting, whether humanly or spiritually. The spiritual experience we need is the kind that persists through ups and downs. Sickness or discouragement may make our experience of life "flat" or "sour," but it does not have to eliminate our having a personal relationship with God or our confidence that he is with us or our making a good spiritualized response to difficult circumstances.

Dry periods are also part of spiritual living. Even though our emotions in relationship to God and spiritual things may seem arid or desiccated, we can still live in a spiritualized way. In fact, it seems to be true that God uses such times to bring us to a new level of spiritual life. A "dry" relationship with God over a period of time, a dry prayer life, forces us to choose whether God himself is more important to us than "what we get out of" prayer or "what we get out of" our spiritual life.

Moreover, as we get older we experience life differently and so experience spiritual life differently. We need an approach to spiritual experience that allows us to be in a good relationship with God when we experience all of life in a quieter, less energetic way. If our model for Christian fervor is the response of a newly converted young person, we will only be able to see our spiritual life as one of steady decline.

We need a broad enough understanding of experience, one that takes in the many ways we experience people and things in the course of human life. Otherwise, we often will be tempted to think that we have lost our relationship with God or at least lost a vital one, despite the fact that the relationship is still there and may even be stronger. Once we come to know the Lord, we should be able to live in the confidence that he is with us and accessible to us despite any ups and downs in our conscious experience of him. It is part of God's plan that we have an experiential relationship with him, one that will sustain us until the point when we enter into the vision of his glory where there will be no room for uncertainty.

THIS GIVES US OUR SECOND CONCLUSION:

Our charismatic spirituality aims at our becoming spiritual(ized) people, people who love God and neighbor with all of our life—for the rest of our life—and are enabled to do that because of an experiential relationship with God.

 CHAPTER THREE

THE WATER OF LIFE

The last two chapters laid a foundation for understanding what the Holy Spirit does in Christians. We first looked at the grace of Pentecost, the "new thing" (Is 43:19, 44:3) that is the basis of the new covenant. God's purpose was to bring into being a people in covenant relationship with him, a people in his image and likeness who loved him and loved one another. As a result of the death and resurrection of Christ, he put his Spirit inside those who believed so that they could fulfill his purpose for the human race.

We then looked at what the gift of the Spirit was supposed to do for us—to make us spiritual or spiritualized people. The gift of the Spirit, viewed corporately or individually, has been given to bring us to what God intended us to be.

We are now going to consider how the Holy Spirit works inside of us. There are two main ways he operates. We might call them "life mode" and "action mode." He gives us life, making us able to live a truly spiritual life, and he works through us to accomplish certain kinds of results. In this chapter we will consider the way he gives us life, and in the next chapter we will look at the way he works through us.

These two chapters will allow us to look at the interaction between the Holy Spirit working in us and our humanity—our capacities and efforts. Devout or pious people, in their desire to emphasize what God does, often denigrate what we do after the Lord has renewed us in him. This can easily lead to the mistaken approach that some have called "hyperspiritualism" or "superspiritualism." In fact, the Holy Spirit works in and through us. He transforms us and our ability to act. He does not annihilate us or replace us, or part of us, or bypass us. We are not supposed to be just passive spectators of our own life in the Spirit but spiritualized people equipped to live for the Lord and serve him by the gift of the Spirit within us.

The Holy Spirit as the Water of Life

The Book of Revelation ends with a vision, often referred to as the vision of the New Jerusalem. It is the vision of what the Lord is aiming at in human history, what he is seeking to bring us to. In explaining the vision the book says:

> Then he showed me the river of the water of life, bright as crystal, flowing from the throne of God and of the Lamb through the middle of the street of the city; also, on either side of the river, the tree of life with its twelve kinds of fruit, yielding its fruit each month; and the leaves of the tree were for the healing of the nations. (Revelation 22:1-2)

Central to this vision is "the river of the water of life" which flows into and through the new Jerusalem.

The water of life comes from the throne of God and of the Lamb. On the throne we see the glory of God shining from the Lamb who is "its lamp" (Rev 21:23). In other words, those who live in the city can see God's throne in their midst, and on that throne is the Lamb of God, our Lord Jesus Christ, filled with divine glory, sharing in his Father's reign over all of creation. The water of life, then, flows from the King of the universe who has died for the redemption of the human race.

The water gives life to the city, "the holy city Jerusalem"

(Rev 21:10). We get heavenly life by being "built into" (Eph 2:22) a temple that is a city, a community of those redeemed by the Lord. The water makes that city into a paradise, a place where the tree of life grows. The water, in other words, restores the Garden of Eden or, better, makes the new Jerusalem into a new Eden, a place where God's original purpose for the human race is fully accomplished.

This is a picture of the end, of what will be. But in a certain way the end is already present now. We are living "in the last days," as Scripture says, and we are already beginning to experience the first installment, or as the RSV translates it, the "guarantee" (Eph 1:14; 2 Cor 5:5), of what is to be given in its fullness after the Lord Jesus comes again. The vision in Revelation, then, reveals to us what will come to pass but also reveals to us something of what we can experience even now.

But what is *the water of life*?

We can find out what the water of life is by looking at a passage in the seventh chapter of the Gospel of John. It is a description of something that happened at the Feast of Tabernacles or Booths in the last year of Jesus' life. During that feast each year there was a ceremony in which water from the Pool of Siloam, at the foot of the mountain spur on which the original Jerusalem was built, was carried in procession to the temple and there poured out to symbolize the redemption that the Lord gives his people. In verses 37-39 we read about what Jesus said, probably right after this ceremony:

> On the last day of the feast, the great day, Jesus stood up and proclaimed, "If anyone thirst, let him come to me and drink, and let him who believes in me drink. As the scripture has said, Out of his heart shall flow rivers of living water." Now this he

> said about the Spirit, which those who believed in him were to
> receive; for as yet the Spirit had not been given, because Jesus
> was not yet glorified.

"His" in this passage probably refers to Christ. If that is so, his heart refers to the heart of Christ. The rivers of living water, then, flow out of the heart of Christ. This passage tells us that it is the Holy Spirit who is the water of life. The Holy Spirit was not given during Jesus' lifetime, but was given when Jesus was glorified, that is, after he died, rose, and ascended to the throne of God in heaven. In other words, the water of life was poured out at Pentecost after the glorification of Jesus. It was given by him once he sat on the throne of God sharing his reign. The picture we get here corresponds closely to the one in Revelation 22, although John presents more strongly the personal connection between the Lord Jesus and the Spirit. Jesus gives us of the Spirit that flows from him personally.

But why water? Where does water as an image of the Holy Spirit come from?

That image goes back to the prophets, especially the prophet Isaiah. We can see it in Isaiah 44. The prophecy concerns a future renewal of the people of Israel, and in verse 3 it says:

> For I will pour water on the thirsty land,
>   and streams on the dry ground;
> I will pour my Spirit upon your descendants,
>   and my blessing on your offspring.

Since this is Hebrew poetry, the lines are parallel, restating in the second half of each verse what was said in the first half. The Lord is saying that he will pour out water or streams in a desert area. Those streams will be the blessing of his Spirit, which he will give to the people of Israel at a future time of restoration.

The image here is of water in a desert, probably at the time of the spring rains. The prophecy is not speaking about a sand desert like the Sahara—the picture that seems to come to mind for most people who do not live in a desert area. The prophecy is referring to a normal arid desert, as is found in Judea on the eastern and southern part of the country.

I had an experience once that allowed me to see vividly what this meant. I was driving in the southern part of Arizona. We were going through normal arid desert, sparsely covered with some cacti and other small desert plants. We drove over a ridge, and all of a sudden there was a completely different scene. The desert was filled with plants of many kinds, all in bloom. It was a glorious sight, even more so because of the contrast with the earlier desert.

We found out later that shortly before we arrived it had rained in the desert, as it does occasionally. In other words, water had been "poured on the thirsty ground." The result was that the desert came to life. Seeds had been waiting in the ground for the water, and once it came they rapidly took advantage of the moisture and grew into plants. It was the water that brought the dry land to life.

The water, however, did not bring dirt to life. If I had dug in that land before, all I would have seen was dirt and pebbles. But some of those pebbles were seeds. They looked dead and in a certain way they were, because they were inert. But they had the potential to be brought to life by the water, and that is what happened. The water came down, and they came to life.

Equally striking was the variety of life. Had I thought about it before that experience, I would almost certainly have thought that there were only a few plants that might live in the desert. But it turned out that there was an abundance of different kinds. Their seeds probably look fairly similar, but the water brought each one to life in accord with the nature it had. If the water touches a hibiscus seed, a hibiscus will grow from that seed, not a cactus.

This is the image we see in Isaiah. The outpouring of the Spirit is like the water that brought that desert to life. The Spirit makes the desert bloom and brings the dead to life. This is one of the prophecies that Jesus was probably referring to when he spoke of the Holy Spirit as the water of life. To say that the Spirit is the water of life is to say that he brings the blessing of life to human beings when poured out upon them.

Now we have to consider what it means to say that the Holy Spirit produces life in us.

The Spirit Gives Life

The last part of the Book of Ephesians (chapters 4-6) is an extended exhortation about how to live the Christian life, based on the truths presented in the first three chapters. The fourth chapter begins with an exhortation to live a life worthy of the Christian call, talks about how the Lord builds up the Christian community, and then talks about the new way of life that should result from redemption in Christ, encouraging the recipients of the letter to live it. In the fifth chapter we come to the following exhortation:

> Look carefully then how you walk, not as unwise men but as wise, making the most of the time, because the days are evil. Therefore do not be foolish, but understand what the will of the Lord is. And do not get drunk with wine, for that is debauchery; but be filled with the Spirit, addressing one another in psalms and hymns and spiritual songs, singing and making melody to the Lord with all your heart, always and for everything giving thanks in the name of our Lord Jesus Christ to God the Father. (Ephesians 5:17-20)

This passage seems to be a simple exhortation to live well. As we read it, however, we come across an exhortation not to "get drunk with wine." If we are paying attention, we might ask ourselves why all of a sudden Paul is concerned with the question of drunkenness. Is he planning on signing up the Ephesians for a temperance movement perhaps?

In fact, he is not especially concerned with drunkenness, but rather he is making a comparison between drinking wine and being filled with the Spirit. Although the words are a little different than the ones we would use, we would speak in a similar way. We talk about people being "tanked." We also talk about their being "under the influence." When people are tanked or "filled with wine," the wine does not just go into them and sit there, as in a bottle. Rather, it enters into the blood stream and "influences" them. They talk differently, walk differently, act differently. We can tell that they have drunk a great deal just by watching them or listening to them.

Something similar happens when someone is "filled with the Spirit." The biblical word *filled* commonly is used to speak about a change in behavior. Someone who is very angry is "filled with anger." The anger determines how the person acts. In a similar way, when we are filled with the Spirit, the Holy Spirit affects our behavior. He does not just go into us and sit there as in a temple so we can worship him. Rather he "enters into our bloodstream." He influences the way we live and act. People should be able to tell that this has happened to us by looking at us or listening to us.

The passage goes on to speak about what happens when the Holy Spirit fills us. We worship the Lord, praising and thanking him. Worship is, in fact, a special sign of the presence of the Holy Spirit in us, as we will see. But the truth has a broader application. The Holy Spirit produces holy living in us, daily life holiness. The teaching here is similar to that in the passage about the fruit of the Spirit. Both make clear that the Holy Spirit produces a new way of "walking" or living, a new kind of behavior. And he does it by working inside of us to make something possible that was not possible before.

Does this mean that when the Holy Spirit fills us we become like drunks or robots or possessed people? Do we lose our ability to think clearly or our capacity to choose what to do? Do we become sub-human in our behavior?

The answer most of us would intuitively and quickly make to these questions is no. The Lord does not make us less human but in a certain way more human. He brings us to life according to our nature. When we are filled with the Spirit, we are more able to understand what is good and to choose it. The Spirit does not make us into automata, determined by God to act in certain ways whether we want to or not, but enables us to act spiritually and so more freely.

We can see something of the way this works by looking at the passage in John chapter 15 where the Lord teaches the parable of the vine:

> I am the true vine, and my Father is the vinedresser....
>
> Abide in me, and I in you. As the branch cannot bear fruit by itself, unless it abides in the vine, neither can you, unless you abide in me. I am the vine, you are the branches. He who abides in me, and I in him, he it is that bears much fruit, for apart from me you can do nothing. If a man does not abide in me, he is cast forth as a branch and withers; and the branches are gathered, thrown into the fire and burned....
>
> As the Father has loved me, so have I loved you; abide in my love. If you keep my commandments, you will abide in my love, just as I have kept my Father's commandments and abide in his love. These things I have spoken to you, that my joy may be in you, and that your joy may be full.

> This is my commandment, that you love one another as I
> have loved you. Greater love has no man than this, that a man
> lay down his life for his friends.... This I command you, to love
> one another. (John 15:1, 4-6, 9-13, 17)

This passage concerns Christ and the way he dwells in human beings, but it refers to the same reality as that of the Holy Spirit dwelling or "abiding" in us. When Christ dwells in us, he dwells in us by the Holy Spirit. Jesus is here comparing himself to a vine and his disciples to the branches of that vine. Together they make up one plant, similar to the way the various members—arms, legs, and so on—make up one body when they are joined with the head.

A vine produces fruit. But we could ask, Whose fruit is it, the vine's or the branch's? The answer is both. This is not an either/or matter. The fruit is fully the vine's fruit and fully the branch's fruit. It makes no sense to say that the fruit is not the branch's fruit or not the vine's fruit.

Saying it that way, however, makes it sound as if the vine and branches are equal partners. That, however, is not true. The vine does not need the branches. The branches can be cut off and the vine will do fine. It may even do better without a given branch or two; that is why we prune vines. But the branches do need the vine. If they are cut off, they die, because they need the vine to stay alive. The vine is the source of their life and the source of their ability to bear fruit.

It is also worth noting that there are certain conditions for the branches [us] to stay alive and bear fruit. We have to keep his commandments. We also have to love one another, the other branches that are part of the same vine. We have, in other words, to live in community or communion with one another and obey the Lord. All of this could be summed up by saying that we need to stay connected or joined with the vine and so "abide in him." To use the language of the first Pentecost, we need to "keep the covenant," because that enables us to be in a living relationship with the Lord.

When God lives in us by joining us to Christ and filling us with his Spirit, he does not make us automata or even simply passive members. We are to be fruit-bearing branches, and if we do not bear fruit, we will be pruned. The Spirit does not by-pass us, but he enables us to do something we could not do be-fore—to bear the fruit of the Spirit. The two passages in Ephesians 5 and John 15 together make clear—and even clearer when we add the Fruit of the Spirit Passage in Galatians 5—that when the Holy Spirit produces life in us, he produces a new way of living, one that we could not produce on our own.

Now, it is true that sometimes God works for us or at our request without working in and through us. When he does so, he gives us special helps. The main way, however, that he wants to work with us is by enabling us, through the spiritual life within, to live effectively as Christians. We can see the differ-ence between God's special help and his ordinary help by con-sidering two examples: healing and having patience. These will show us two models of the way God works.

We can begin with prayer for healing. Suppose that we see someone sick. We might decide that we should pray for that person to get healed. Then he or she might get healed right away as the result of our prayer.

This is not the same thing as what happens when a doctor heals someone. Doctors go through medical school and intern-ship. They acquire a great deal of knowledge and skill by hard work and training. They then work at getting people healed: examining them, diagnosing their problems, prescribing remedies, possibly operating on them, checking back with them to see how various remedies have worked, and so on. When they heal someone, they make use of an acquired ability to bring about health, and they usually can tell how they did what they did.

When we pray for someone and the person gets healed, we are not relying on an acquired ability. Rather, we are relying on something outside of ourselves—namely, the Lord. We are asking him to do something we ourselves cannot do, and we are possibly asking him to do something that would not happen— or might not happen for a long time—if he did not act.

We are not completely irrelevant in this instance. If we did not pray, likely the person would not be healed, at least not now. But rather than accomplishing the healing ourselves, we are acting like a conduit of something outside ourselves—the healing action of God. It would be appropriate and accurate to say that God did this, not we.

Now let us consider patience and courage, both fruits of the Spirit. Suppose that we are at the breakfast table, and our young son spills his milk all over us once again. How do we respond? Do we reprimand him because we are irritated? Do we spank him so that he learns not to do it again? Or do we say he is too young to do better so we should just have patience and overlook it? Suppose the latter is the appropriate response. Then we just need to have patience.

At such a point, it would be nice if God would have patience for us or instead of us. It would be nice if we could just "yield to the Spirit" and relax, or "let go and let God" as the old charismatic motto had it.

Of course, if we let go, we would be very likely to reprimand our son, whether that would be the best thing to do or not. Instead we need to exercise self-control or patience, sometimes with great effort. And we probably should be grateful if we have acquired the ability to do that over the years rather than relying on praying to God for special emergency help because we never did grow in patience.

A number of years ago I read a newspaper account of a man who saved a woman from rape in the subway in New York. To understand the incident, you should know that the platforms of the subway stations there are lit up where the passengers stand to board the trains, but the lights extend only slightly into the tunnel, ending in complete darkness further along. The man described how he was waiting for a train and then heard a muffled scream. He looked over and could see two figures in the shadows, one a woman and the other a very large man who seemed to have a weapon. He looked around, hoping to see a policeman, but there was no one else on the platform.

He decided then that since he was the only one who could help, he had to try, even though it looked to him as if he would be getting himself into some very serious trouble and perhaps killed. He looked at the scene, and fear filled him. What should he do? Respond by "letting go and letting God"? If he had let go, he probably would have run the other way as quickly as he could. He actually said, "I decided I had to run to help the woman, and God helped me."

Now, this is a story with a happy ending. The assailant heard him and ran away—"luckily for me," as the man telling the story said. Despite his fear, he needed to act with courage, and he did. He was apparently a Christian, because he recognized that God was at work in him in the situation. He did not, however, stand back and "let God work" or just pray. He acted with courage—and God worked.

For many of those involved in the charismatic renewal, the sole model for the action of God is something like praying for healing. When we pray or just do nothing and rely on God to act, that is when God really can act. But that is only one model of how God acts, the model that emphasizes human passivity. It leaves out the fact that God often acts in and through us when we act. Sometimes he does that by strengthening us so that we develop the fruit of the Spirit, as when we patiently handle a child causing trouble. Sometimes we just do what we can, as when the man ran to help the woman, and God uses what we do to get something to happen.

This second model of how God works, his working when we are ourselves doing what we can, is the ordinary one. In God's plan it is the more common one, because God wants to make us spiritual people, capable of handling the ordinary circumstances of life in a good way. He needs to give us special help at times. At times he even seems to want to give us special help just to show us that he is present or to make things happen that are beyond our power. But the ordinary, normal, or basic help God gives to those who belong to his Son is to work in them to act in a better way.

The failure to understand the difference between special helps and the basic help that God gives us can cause us to remain spiritually immature. The best description of the dynamics of spiritual maturity can be found in Hebrews 5:14: "But solid food is for the mature, for those who have their faculties trained by practice to distinguish good from evil."

This verse is part of an explanation why the author is not going to give basic instruction (something like a Sunday school or catechism lesson) again, even though it might seem that his audience needs it. He will not give them teaching that is like milk for babies. He will give them the teaching that is like solid food for grown-ups.

To understand the difference between being a baby and a mature person, we can consider the example of the human arm. A newborn child has an arm at birth, and that arm is a gift of God, something the newborn baby could not have acquired by any efforts of its own, any more than it could get itself born. However, the newborn child cannot do much with that arm. If we say, for instance, that human beings can use their arms to throw balls, that would be a true statement, but it would not apply to the baby.

The newborn child needs to use his arm over the years before he can throw balls. Even more, he has to train his arm if he is going to become good at throwing balls. For his arm to become the arm of an adult, even more the arm of an athlete, he needs "training by practice" over years.

Hebrews 5:14 gives us a criterion for what it is to be mature as a Christian. The result of Christian maturity is the ability to distinguish good from evil. We can see from the context that the author is not just speaking about the ability to know the difference between good and evil theoretically—that is, the ability to know that patience is good and impatience bad, or perhaps the ability to give a definition of patience. Rather, he is speaking about the ability to know how to act in a good way rather than a bad way in the various situations in life that we confront (like the one his audience is confronting), an ability that we might describe as good judgment. Someone who is mature as a parent should be able to tell when to discipline a child and when to let something go and be patient because the child cannot do any better—for the most part at least.

We gain this ability by *practice*. Maturity in Christian living, mature Christian character, develops through practice. "Practiced" character allows us to know in each situation, more or less instinctively, what is good or bad. As a result of experience and practice, we are *trained* in responding well, developing good judgment as well as skill in acting well. The word *trained* here comes from athletics. We need to train as an athlete does to have Christian maturity, not just learn about it in a book. Growth in maturity, then, involves hard work that is made possible by something God gives but that needs development.

Christian discipleship training, then, needs to follow on spiritual birth if we are to become mature Christians, Christians who can handle the various situations in life the way they should. Failure to understand this leaves one in a state of Christian immaturity. Sometimes that failure is rooted in having only one model of how God acts, the way he acts when he gives us special help, and consequently failing to acquire a formation that allows us to develop the fruit of the Spirit, which works on a different model.

We sometimes use the word *hyperspiritualism* or *superspiritualism*. Hyperspiritualism is the problem of looking to God to bypass the human rather than transform it, and so to expect things to happen by the power of the Spirit without human cooperation more often than is good. People who are suffering from hyperspiritualism miss the fact that we are supposed to be transformed by the presence of the Spirit in us and so live in a spiritualized way. We are supposed to live like human beings—think, decide, act, work, and persevere—but to have our human faculties or actions formed so that they express the character of God. We should be able to handle more and more situations as the Lord would rather than constantly looking to God to bypass us, to handle difficult situations without us or instead of us.

Hyperspiritualism is not just a matter of overemphasis. It is a depreciation, sometimes conscious, sometimes de facto, of an aspect of the way the Spirit works. We can, in principle, maximize both the spiritual and the good human at the same time. It is not true that if something is spiritual, it does not come from human effort, any more than it is true that if the fruit comes from the vine, it does not come from the branches. Both can work together. It is the unredeemed human, not everything human, that is incompatible with the spiritual.

There are limits to this, of course. When we want to see someone healed, we can pray and God may act without human effort. Sometimes that is the only way, or the best way, to get something to happen. Nonetheless, if that is our only model for the way God acts and we want to be spiritual people who rely upon God, we may fall into hyperspiritualism and become less effective as Christians. The main way God wants to work is by spiritualizing us, transforming us, so that we become the kind of people who can live and act in a spiritual way.

"Bucket Faith" and "Spring Faith"

The Gospel of John gives us a picture of the kind of faith that is a response to the new life the Holy Spirit gives us—"spring faith." We can read about it in the fourth chapter, where Jesus has a discussion with the Samaritan woman at Jacob's well in the land of Samaria:

Interchange 1

There came a woman of Samaria to draw water. Jesus said to her, "Give me a drink." For his disciples had gone away into the city to buy food. The Samaritan woman said to him, "How is it that you, a Jew, ask a drink of me, a woman of Samaria?" For Jews have no dealings with Samaritans. Jesus answered her, "If you knew the gift of God, and who it is that is saying to you, 'Give me a drink,' you would have asked him, and he would have given you living water."

Interchange 2

The woman said to him, "Sir, you have nothing to draw with, and the well is deep; where do you get that living water? Are you greater than our father Jacob, who gave us the well, and drank from it himself, and his sons, and his cattle?" Jesus said to her, "Every one who drinks of this water will thirst again, but whoever drinks of the water that I shall give him will never

thirst; the water that I shall give him will become in him a
spring of water welling up to eternal life." (John 4:7-14)

The passage itself gives us background. It tells us that Jesus'
disciples had gone into the nearby city to buy food, and while
he was waiting for them at the well, a Samaritan woman came
to draw water. The passage also tells us that Jews had no dealings with Samaritans. That, however, is not the best translation,
as we can see from the fact that the disciples had gone into the
nearby Samaritan city to buy food, certainly some kind of a
"dealing" with Samaritans. A better translation is "Jews do not
use vessels with Samaritans." Jews thought the Samaritans did
not observe purity laws properly, and as a result, a drinking
vessel handled by a Samaritan woman was likely to be unclean
and so should be avoided.

The issue, then, concerned maintaining ceremonial purity
and not simply avoiding Samaritans completely. Nor was it a
matter of not speaking to women, as some authors assert to try
to make the point that Jesus was more liberal than other Jews
were in terms of dealing with women. It was a matter of not
using a vessel that could have been made ritually impure by a
Samaritan woman. Nonetheless, Jesus asked the Samaritan
woman for a drink from her bucket.

The woman responded in an unfriendly manner. She
wanted to know why he was doing something he was not supposed to do. Rather than give her an answer that she could understand as a response to her question, Jesus said, "If you knew
the gift of God, and who it is that is saying to you, 'Give me a
drink,' you would have asked him, and he would have given
you living water."

"Living water" is the literal translation of the phrase used.
"Flowing water" is an alternate translation. Flowing water was
described as living water because it moved, in contrast to
the water in a well or cistern. Probably the Samaritan woman

understood Jesus to be speaking about flowing water, because she replied that the only water in the area was well water, water from Jacob's well. Moreover, he could not even get that water, because he had nothing to draw with, no bucket, and the well was deep.

In using the phrase *living water,* of course, Jesus was making a play on words. The water Jesus had to give was flowing but also alive. It was, moreover, *the* gift of God.

The woman's reply to Jesus' claim to have flowing (living) water to give was even more sarcastic than her first response. She was in effect saying, "How come you talk so big, when you cannot get yourself a drink of water?" She also recognized that he was implicitly making a claim that he had better water than Jacob's well contained, and she added, "The well was good enough for Jacob, how come it is not good enough for you? Are you such an important person?"

Jesus responded, "I do not give just drinks of water. I give water that stays inside and will be a spring of water inside of people. Moreover, that spring will make it possible for them to have eternal life."

As we can see from what he said later on in his discussion with the Samaritan woman, this "spring of water" refers to the presence of the Holy Spirit in those who receive him from the Lord. He is speaking about the gift of God, the promise of the Father. This presence of the Holy Spirit is intended by God to be an ongoing presence in us, giving us spiritual life until it brings us to where we should be—to heaven, to eternal life.

Using the image in this passage, we can distinguish between "bucket faith" and "spring faith." Bucket faith is the kind that looks for divine help outside of us. At times we need to look for help from God we do not have, to "get a bucket" and go after it. Spring faith relies on help from God we have already been given. It relies on the gift inside that does not go away.

To be sure, the life the Lord gives us needs to be fed at times. We need "word and sacrament," or "Liturgy of the Word and Liturgy of the Eucharist," to use the theological phrases. We also need to have the channel cleaned out at times. We need to repent and seek forgiveness. Nonetheless, the life and strength that comes to us when we are joined to Christ is already inside of us and remains there unless something goes radically wrong.

This is where spring faith comes in. Spring faith relies on the spring of living water inside. It lives and acts in the confidence that the Holy Spirit is inside of us and is there to enlighten us and strengthen us so that we can handle the various circumstances of our life in a good Christian way.

If we are, for instance, raising a family, there are many times when we will want to get out our bucket and go for help. We may be financially responsible, but we now need more money than we did in the past. We may have acquired much good Christian teaching and help so that we mainly know what we need to do, but now we do not have a clue how to handle something that happened to one of our children, or we cannot explain a sudden turn for the worse in his or her life that the child will not talk about. Going to the Lord for special help may be needed.

But our family life will go much better (and probably will have fewer special needs) if we learn to rely upon the fact that the Lord is in us. We can handle difficulties and learn how to be a parent if we have confidence that we can rely on the Lord at work inside of us. We are his sons and daughters, filled with his Spirit, holding a privileged position. If we live and act with that confidence, with spring faith in the gift of the Lord in us, we will see a better life and better results. Spring faith does not guarantee that everything will go well, but it makes a significant difference.

Spring faith does not always work best by "claiming God's help in faith" whenever we need it. We do not need to claim something we already have. We need to do that when we use bucket faith to get special help. Spring faith is rather an ongoing confidence in the Lord, one that is nourished day in and day out by remembering who we are, who God is, and what our relationship with God is like—what he has already given us. Sometimes spring faith works best when it is instinctive, when we simply act with the confidence of who we are in the Lord.

THIS GIVES US OUR THIRD CONCLUSION:

Our charismatic spirituality is based upon confidence that the Holy Spirit is in us and transforms, enlightens, and strengthens us so that we can be spiritual(ized) people.

 CHAPTER FOUR

GIFTS AND GRACES

The Holy Spirit is the life-giver (see 2 Cor 3:6). But he does not just give us life; he also works in us and through us. In the last chapter we considered the way in which the Holy Spirit dwells in us and works inside of us to give us life and the fruit that comes from that life. We are now going to consider the way he works through us so that we can act more effectively to advance the kingdom of God.

This is not a chapter on the spiritual gifts, the gifts listed in 1 Corinthians 12:8-10 and referred to in other scriptural texts. It will mention them but not go into what they are and how they function. It presupposes some understanding of those gifts, which are commonly taught about in writings on charismatic renewal. Nor is the focus on "stirring up" particular spiritual gifts. Rather, the chapter focuses on acting confidently as servants of the Lord who have been gifted by him.

Many who have read treatments of the gifts of the Holy Spirit have been given one of two orientations. One is what some have called the "apostle's-eye view" of such gifts. This one is easy to fall into inadvertently, because the greatest single source of scriptural discussion on gifts and graces is the apostle Paul, and he often spoke about them when he was talking about his own experience. The second orientation is the "conference and prayer meeting orientation," which comes from the fact that the presentations given are intended to help people participate well (and "charismatically") in conferences and prayer meetings.

Both orientations have their uses, but they are too limited to provide an overall view of the gifts and graces of the Spirit that equip us to act and serve as Christians. This chapter will instead give what could be called a "daily life orientation," because the focus will be on how the Holy Spirit works in us for all of our lives.

The "Breath" of God

We tend to think of the Spirit as being immaterial (a true statement) and therefore weaker, less substantial (a false one). Psalm 33:6-9 makes it clear that something spiritual is something powerful, something "charged with" the Spirit, who is the power of God:

> By the word of the LORD the heavens were made,
>   and all their host by the breath of his mouth.
> He gathered the waters of the sea as in a bottle;
>   he put the deeps in storehouses.
>
> Let all the earth fear the LORD,
>   let all the inhabitants of the world stand in awe of him!
> For he spoke, and it came to be;
>   he commanded, and it stood forth.

The word *Spirit* is a translation of a Hebrew (and Greek) word that sometimes is translated "breath," as in the above psalm, and at other times, "wind." The Holy Spirit, then, is "the breath of his [God's] mouth."

There is an image behind the use of *word* and *spirit* as synonyms in this psalm. We can only speak a word when we breathe out. To speak, we breathe and form our breath into a sound of a certain sort. A word then comes into existence. The breath (spirit) gives the force or energy for the word to be spoken and heard. If you project your voice or shout, you realize this more quickly, because doing so takes more breath.

The word of God creates heaven and earth. Speaking of "the heavens ... and all their host ..." as well as "the earth ... and all the inhabitants of the world," the psalm says, "He spoke, and it came to be; he commanded, and it stood forth." In other words, by speaking a command, God created everything. His command contained the understanding of what he wanted to happen, which came from his wisdom or reason. His breath or spirit contained the force or power that brought it into existence. The Spirit with which he breathes his word is creative power itself.

Although seemingly insubstantial, wind can be very powerful. We can see something of this by considering a hurricane or tornado, both very strong winds. I was once staying with my mother when she lived close to Miami on Biscayne Boulevard. One evening a tornado decided to go north on Biscayne Boulevard. It touched down at three points and then headed out to sea. The next morning I went to one of the spots where it had landed and was impressed with how little it left of what once was a substantial building. The Scripture tells us that this is the kind of power that the "breath of God" has.

On the other hand, wind can have constructive effects. It can blow on a windmill and produce electricity or power a water pump. It can fill sails and move a boat across a great ocean. To get such results, we need the ability to receive the wind and apply its power to something useful.

Sometimes we use the phrase "charged with the Spirit." Behind this is the image of an electrical wire. We can plug a cord into an appliance and nothing will happen. When, however, the other end of the cord is plugged into a socket, the cord is charged with electricity and brings electrical power into the appliance to enable it to function. Something charged with the Spirit is spiritually powerful and capable of getting spiritual results.

Spirit, then, is something forceful or powerful. The Holy Spirit, the holy breath of God or wind from God, brings with him God's power. He enables what he enters into to operate with spiritual or divine power. That is why Jesus said in Acts 1:8, "But you shall receive power when the Holy Spirit has come upon you," and why Peter said in Acts 10:38, "God anointed Jesus of Nazareth with the Holy Spirit and with power."

The Holy Spirit, however, is not naked power or brute force. He brings power accompanied by and formed by wisdom, because he is the power of God. As a consequence, he not only seeks to make our action more powerful, he also seeks to direct our action so that we know better what to do and how to do it. When the apostles wanted to choose what are sometimes described as the first deacons (servants), Peter said to the community, "Therefore, brethren, pick out from among you seven men of good repute, full of the Spirit and of wisdom [or full of the Spirit of wisdom, the wisdom-bringing Spirit], whom we may appoint to this duty" (Acts 6:3). They were to look for men to whom the Holy Spirit had given wisdom, spiritually wise men. It is the combination of wisdom and power that forms human action and makes it effective and not chaotic or destructive, like that of an enraged man out of control. When we receive the Holy Spirit, then, he enters into us with wisdom and power, to equip us and work through us so that we can serve the kingdom of God in a more effective way.

Gifts and Graces We Can Expect

Scripture speaks about gifts and graces that come from God, to use the traditional English translations. The two words seem to be rough synonyms, although some teachers distinguish between them. They are used to speak about what God does inside of us when he takes us into relationship with himself and fills us with his Spirit. They are called gifts or graces (favors), because they are not something we can earn or acquire by our own efforts, like the skill attested by a medical degree, but are the result of the Holy Spirit working in us "as he wills."

On the other hand, gifts and graces of the Holy Spirit are not like modern birthday gifts but are more like birthday gifts used to be. I remember that when I was a child, I received toys or something similar from most people, but I could always count on my aunt, who was a somewhat old-fashioned person, to provide me with some clothing or something else "useful." My parents seemed happier with her gift than I was.

God's gifts, at least for the most part, are not given to us to enjoy or use for whatever we want. I once visited a park that had belonged to a duke in England. They showed us where "the lion" had been kept, a place surrounded by a strong fence. Some tribal chief in Africa had apparently sent the duke a lion as a gift. The gift, however, had a mind of its own, so there were only a very limited number of things the duke could do with him. God's gifts are more like having a lion than having a gift certificate—they have "a mind of their own," so to speak. We can only make use of them if we cooperate with the way they function.

The word *gifts* can also be misleading in another way. When we think of a gift, we think of something we can take and carry off and still make use of when the giver is gone. But the gifts of the Spirit, especially the charismatic gifts or spiritual gifts, do not function apart from the giver himself. They are ways to receive the action of the Spirit working in and through us to accomplish some purpose that we can only serve.

On the other hand, a gift of the Spirit is not exactly the same thing as a particular action of the Spirit or a working of the Spirit. In 1 Corinthians 12 Paul discussed "spiritual things" (a phrase the RSV translates as "spiritual gifts") like the gifts of tongues, prophecy, healing, and miracles, which he described as "manifestations of the Spirit" (verse 7). He discussed them in order to put them into a context that would allow the Corinthians to understand how to respond to them well.

In verses 4-6 he began to speak directly of these gifts: "Now there are varieties of gifts, but the same Spirit; and there are varieties of service, but the same Lord; and there are varieties of working, but it is the same God who inspires them all in every one." Paul here uses three terms: *gifts*, *services*, and *workings*. The last word is difficult to translate but is sometimes rendered "operation" or "inspiration." It is used to describe the fact that God at times works through us (operates through us) to get something to happen.

These three words all refer to the same set of things, but they have three somewhat different meanings. When people are "healers," God works through them to heal, and so the healing that occurs is a work of God. At the same time, by praying for people, healers are performing a service. But also they have been given a gift that enables them to receive the workings of God that allow them to perform their service.

Having a "gift" can be distinguished from experiencing or cooperating with a "working," as being a prophet or having the gift to be a prophet can be distinguished from giving a prophecy. The working is God's action, God's doing something through us. The gift is God's having enabled us to receive his working on a regular basis. God seems willing to work through a great variety of people to heal at different times. But if we speak of someone as having the gift of healing, we mean more than that. We mean that that person can somehow tap into the working of God in a regular way and so can get more regular results than someone who just prays over another person and sees a healing.

We can, then, see the gifts and graces of the Spirit as equipping us or "programming" us, making us "spiritual receptors." To use an analogy, the internet can send music. But if we do not have an application or program on our computer that is capable of receiving what is sent, we will never hear that music. When the Holy Spirit gives us gifts, he does something like program us—that is, change us spiritually inside—so that we can receive what he does, his "workings," in an ongoing way.

The remainder of this chapter will provide an overview of the three main kinds of gifts the Holy Spirit gives, concentrating on the charismatic or ministry gifts.

The Gift of the Spirit Himself

The first kind of gift that we receive is one that we have already discussed, the gift of the Spirit himself. This is the chief gift we are given. When we have received the gift of the Spirit, we have God himself abiding in us, giving us life and working in and through us.

As we have seen, the gift of the Spirit brings us new life, and as a result of that life, the fruits of the Spirit should grow. To be sure, life needs feeding and this fruit comes through exercise or practice. Some people who have received the Spirit or been baptized in the Spirit do not seem to have received much spiritual life or to have become very spiritualized. Nonetheless, spiritual life and the fruit of the Spirit become possible, in principle, through the gift of the Spirit.

The life-giving presence of the Holy Spirit in us makes it

possible for us to be effective. If we were not alive, we could not do anything. Therefore, without the spiritual life the Holy Spirit gives, we cannot do anything or have any effect as Christians. However, considering the gift of new life in the Spirit and the way he works to enable us to develop greater likeness to God in our character does not cover all his gifts. He also gives us gifts that equip us to be effective in serving him or in acting to advance his kingdom, and those are the focus of this chapter. Here we do not need to do any more than call to mind the basic gift of the Spirit so that we can see the overview.

Gifts and Graces for All

Some gifts of the Spirit seem to be for everyone, the kind of spiritual equipment that comes with being a Christian. The prophecy in Isaiah 11:1-5 has been traditionally understood to be a description of such gifts:

> There shall come forth a shoot from the stump of Jesse,
>   and a branch shall grow out of his roots.
> And the Spirit of the LORD shall rest upon him,
>   the spirit of wisdom and understanding,
>   the spirit of counsel and might,
>   the spirit of knowledge and the fear of the LORD
> And his delight shall be in the fear of the LORD.
>
> He shall not judge by what his eyes see,
>   or decide by what his ears hear;
> but with righteousness he shall judge the poor,
>   and decide with equity for the meek of the earth;
> and he shall smite the earth with the rod of his mouth,
>   and with the breath of his lips he shall slay the wicked.
> Righteousness shall be the girdle of his waist,
>   and faithfulness the girdle of his loins.

This is a prophecy about the coming Messiah, delivered toward the end of the eighth century B.C. The royal house of Judah, the house of David, here referred to by mentioning Jesse, the father of David, is like a large tree that has been cut down. Only the stump remains. But a new shoot or branch will grow out of it. That shoot will be the Messiah, that is, an anointed king. In other words, at a time when it will look as if there are no kings left, a new king will arise.

According to the prophecy, this promised Messiah will have the Holy Spirit rest on him—that is, come into him in an abiding way in order to equip him to be an effective king. The same thing, in other words, will happen to this descendant of David that was described in 1 Samuel 16:13 as happening to David himself: "Then Samuel took the horn of oil, and anointed him in the midst of his brothers; and the Spirit of the Lord came mightily upon David from that day forward."

In other words, David was anointed by Samuel to be the king, and then the Spirit of the Lord came upon him in a powerful way to equip him to be king. The Spirit needed to remain with him and work through him in an ongoing way, because he was to be king for over forty years, all day long and all year long. David did not receive a particular working (inspiration) or help when he was anointed but a spiritual equipping that lasted "from that day forward."

According to the prophecy, the Holy Spirit would provide different kinds of spiritual equipment for this king and, as we shall see, for us. There are some different interpretations of the set of words that describe this equipment, but the following is a helpful one:

Wisdom and understanding: These correspond to what we might call mental formation, the mental formation that allows us to know basic truths like the nature of God, the creation of the world, and basic morality—that is, what is right and wrong. A king who has these gifts should be able to understand what he is about in the light of an overall grasp of the world and its relationship to God, of human life and how it can arrive at what God created it to be. The Spirit of God works in us to teach us, to so form our minds that we can understand foundational truths in a spiritualized way.

Counsel and might: These are equipment for action. *Counsel* is good judgment about what to do as different situations present themselves to us. *Might* is the strength to do what we need to do, especially the ability to handle difficulties or obstacles that might turn us away from doing what we judge is the right thing to do. The Spirit of God works in us to make us effective servants (agents) of his.

Knowledge and fear of the Lord: These concern our relationship with God. *Knowledge* in this context probably refers to the personal experiential knowledge of God and what he wants of us. It is "knowing him and not just knowing about him." *Fear of the Lord* is obedience to him. The Spirit of God works in us so that we can be in a good relationship with God.

His delight is the fear of the Lord seems to be a concluding summary statement. A godly king should be someone who delights to do what God wants, whose inner orientation is to do what God wants in everything. David was described as a "man after [God's] own heart" (1 Sm 13:14), not meaning that God had affection for him but that David wanted what God wanted. The Spirit of God works in us so that we can be a people after God's own heart.

According to the prophecy, this equipment would allow the Messiah to judge and decide as well as to smite and slay. In other words, he was to be equipped to function as a king, a godly king. Revelation 19:11, the description of the ultimate fulfillment of the prophecy in Isaiah 11:1-5, says something similar about the king who is the Word of God: "In righteousness he judges and makes war." He exercises, in other words, the two main functions of kings in the ancient world—judgment or administration of justice and leading in war. He does so effectively with the help of the Spirit of God and in righteousness and faithfulness, the character of God, which is bestowed by the Spirit of God.

The king is a leader in war and engages in combat with the enemy. The enemy, according to the prophecy, is "the wicked." We know from Paul that the true enemy is "the spiritual hosts of wickedness in heavenly places" (Eph 6:12). The true war will be fought against Satan and his kingdom, and the king will primarily fight by his word, "the rod of his mouth."

This is a prophecy about the Messiah, and it was fulfilled when Christ came. Many of the fathers of the church saw this as fulfilled at Christ's baptism, when the Holy Spirit rested upon him. Irenaeus, a second-century father, described the Spirit in his book *Against the Heretics* (III, 17) as "the Holy Spirit, who descended upon the Lord, *the spirit of wisdom and understanding, the spirit of counsel and fortitude, the spirit of knowledge and piety, the spirit of the fear of the Lord,* and whom he in turn gave to the Church, sending the Paraclete from heaven unto all the earth." Irenaeus saw the seven "gifts" as seven ways in which the Holy Spirit himself operates in us. The prophecy in Isaiah 11, then, was fulfilled when the Holy Spirit descended upon the Lord to equip him to save us and to bring the kingdom of God to the human race (see also Lk 4:16-21).

But it was also poured out on him for us, so that when we are baptized and baptized with the Spirit, we too are equipped as he was.

Isaiah 11, then, lists a set of gifts that are poured out upon the Messiah and through him on his followers. This is a different list from that of the fruits of the Spirit in Galatians 5. The difference in the two lists has given rise to discussions about the difference between the "seven gifts" of Isaiah and the nine (or twelve, for those who use the Latin translation) "fruits of the Spirit." Some see no difference between them or link them together in various ways.

If, however, we look at the purpose of the two passages, it is reasonable to see the seven gifts of Isaiah as equipment so that we can act more effectively, "reign with Christ," serve with him for the advancement of the kingdom of God. At the same time, the fruits of the Spirit are the basic character traits or patterns of behavior that allow us to be people who love God and neighbor and so live and act like Christ. The Spirit gives rise to both, but in doing so he is trying to achieve two somewhat different, although related, goals. Both can be seen as intrinsically linked to the gift of the Spirit himself, accomplishing the purpose of the Lord in giving the Spirit, that is, making us effective spiritual(ized) people.

God, then, gives certain gifts to all of us. He allows us to participate in the gifts that Christ, the Messiah, was given so that he could advance the kingdom of God in the face of spiritual opposition. We all therefore have been equipped with gifts that allow us to receive and grow in spiritual wisdom and understanding, so we can understand basic truths about reality and morality; counsel and might, so we can act more effectively; and knowledge and fear of the Lord, so we can be in good relationship with the Lord. We can be people whose delight is in the fear of the Lord so that we live as his servants, to advance his will and his kingdom. If we have confidence that God has done these things in us, we will be able to advance his kingdom more effectively.

Gifts and Graces for Various Services

All the above is given to the Christian people corporately as the body of Christ. When we are built into God's temple so that we can be a dwelling place for his Spirit (Eph 2:22), the gifts are given to us individually. Now we turn to consider gifts that are given to individual members but that vary from person to person. These are given to equip us for different services in the Christian community.

Here again there is a variety in the use of terms that can be confusing. In English writings these gifts are sometimes called "charisms," sometimes "charismatic gifts," sometimes "ministry (service) gifts." In what follows we will use the term "ministry gift" because it makes prominent the fact that the Lord gives us such gifts to equip us for a particular service or services. It is based on a Pauline usage—the Greek word *diakonia*, which is often translated "ministry" in English.

We can helpfully distinguish a ministry gift from a "particular working" of the Spirit. Some people are prophets or have a gift of prophecy and therefore also have a ministry or service of prophecy. As a result they give prophecies, and when they do so, God works through them to speak to his people. The giving of a true prophecy is a particular working of the Spirit.

Some people, however, only prophesy once, like the seventy elders of Israel (see Nm 11:25), or only occasionally. They do not seem to have the ministry gift of prophecy, but they do experience the particular working of prophecy from time to time. We will, then, use the term "particular working" for any time that the Lord works through people, whether they have a gift to receive that working in an ongoing way or only experience it once or occasionally. We will speak of "ministry gift" as the way God equips someone to do a service for him in an ongoing way.[1]

Scripture speaks of gifts and graces as things people "have" and "use" (1 Pt 4:10). They can even be stirred up or "rekindled" if they have been neglected (2 Tm 1:6; 1 Tm 4:14). If people have them and can use them or stir them up, such gifts and graces must be some kind of ability or equipment that stays with them. These passages, then, are not referring just to a particular working that happens but may never happen again or may happen only rarely. Seeing them only as particular workings or inspirations does not give us a full picture, because it leaves out what has happened to people to make it possible for God to work through them. They have been given ministry gifts.

One ministry gift can involve more than one kind of spiritual working. As we have seen, the ministry gift of which we have the fullest picture in Scripture is the gift to be an apostle, because Paul often described his own functioning as an apostle. Paul said in 2 Corinthians 12:12 of his visit to the Corinthians, "The signs of a true apostle were performed among you in all patience, with signs and wonders and mighty works."

---

[1] Very often when people speak about "spiritual gifts," they focus on particular workings of the Spirit. Most contemporary books on spiritual gifts seem to concentrate on particular workings, not on ministries or the gifts to perform those ministries. The term *spiritual gift* seems to come from the King James Version translation of a word found in 1 Corinthians 12:1 and 14:1 that means "spiritual thing." It could, in fact, be translated "spiritual working." There is a well-grounded scholarly opinion that understands the subject matter of 1 Corinthians 12–14 as being workings of a more manifestly supernatural sort and sees Paul as seeking to teach the Corinthians that such workings are to be approached as ministry gifts, to build up the body.

Paul worked miracles and healed people, but he was not a healer or miracle worker. He was an apostle, and he viewed the fact that God worked through him to produced miracles as an indication that he was a true apostle. God worked through him by several spiritual workings that were needed to perform the ministry he was given.

There are a number of scriptural texts that instruct us in the ministry gifts of the Spirit. The most important of these, the ones in which ministry gifts are not just referred to but are the subject of the passage, are Ephesians 4:1-16; Romans 12:3-6; 1 Corinthians 12-14; 1 Peter 4:10-11. Giving an exposition of these texts would take too long for a book like this, so we will try to put together an overall picture out of these texts. We will also presuppose a basic understanding of how the particular gifts mentioned function.

Gifts in a body. The passages in Ephesians 4, Romans 12 and 1 Corinthians 12-14 use the image of a body with many members to help people understand a Christian church or community operating by various ministry gifts. We can see this in the Ephesians text:

> But grace was given to each of us according to the measure of Christ's gift....
>
> And his gifts were that some should be apostles, some prophets, some evangelists, some pastors and teachers, to equip the saints for the work of ministry for building up the body of Christ, until we all attain to the unity of the faith and of the knowledge of the Son of God, to mature manhood, to the measure of the stature of the fullness of Christ; so that we may no longer be children, tossed to and fro and carried about with every wind of doctrine, by the cunning of men, by their craftiness in deceitful wiles.
>
> Rather, speaking the truth in love, we are to grow up in every way into him who is the head, into Christ, from whom the whole body, joined and knit together by every joint with which

> it is supplied, when each part is working properly, makes bodily
> growth and upbuilds itself in love. (Ephesians 4:7, 11-16)

There are some different understandings of this passage.
Probably the best one is that the passage is addressing a missionary situation, that of a newly formed community. It seems
to take the view that in order to grow, new communities normally need to have traveling workers come to build them up
and fully establish them. That means that the passage, when it
speaks about the result (vv. 12-15), is primarily speaking about
the body as a whole. It is speaking of the community, not the
individual Christian, as needing to grow up—although, of
course, individual Christians have their own need to grow into
maturity. This understanding also implies that the list of gifts in
verse 11 refers to missionary ministries: the ministries of traveling apostles, prophets, teachers, and evangelists—all of whom
came to various locations and helped to start and establish new
communities but probably did not normally settle there.

The picture we get of the final product at the end of the
passage is of a *whole body*, built up by many members, each of
which has a different function than the others, with all linked
together. The result is that the community as a whole "makes
bodily growth and builds itself up in love"—that is, in a life of
love of God and love of neighbor. A Christian community, in
short, needs to arrive at the point where it can build itself up in
a stable, ongoing way.

For this to happen, all the *parts*—that is, all the members—
have to *work properly*. They need to serve in a different way
than other members and serve well. They therefore need some
grace that equips them to serve. Those graces differ and fit the
different members to take different roles in the functioning of
the body. The comparison of the community to the human body
provides a guiding image of the gifts and graces the Lord gives
for ministry as equipment. These gifts and graces equip the

members of a community to play differing parts in the life of the community but also to function together in an effective way.

Most commonly we think of ministry gifts as operating in the context of meetings (conferences, prayer meetings, church services) or in the context of church or community activities. That was not, however, the view in the New Testament. New Testament writers did not think in terms of a modern religious organization or of modern churches—which largely function as religious organizations—but of a Christian community, a body of people who interacted together outside of corporate events and shared a common way of life. That probably means that they saw the various ministry gifts, most of them at least, as operating in the course of daily life.

Gifts for daily life. To see that ministry gifts can and probably should work in daily life ways, we have to free ourselves from certain models of how they work. We especially have to free ourselves from focusing on the more manifestly supernatural gifts. Such a focus leads us to think of ministry gifts as connected with special events rather than ordinary life.

There is a scale of "manifestness" or "obvious supernaturality" or "miraculousness" of God's gifts when they operate. Not all of what God does through us is very obviously supernatural. Therefore, many of the results of his work are not manifestly God at work. They usually seem as if they could come from merely natural human efforts, but that does not mean they are not the result of special workings of God.

For instance, someone might give a prophecy that predicts the eruption of a volcano a week ahead of time, as may have happened in the case of the eruption of Mount Helena. That same person might give an especially apropos prophecy to someone being prayed over by a group of people, even though the prophet did not know much about the person or the circumstances. The former would be much more manifestly something that God was involved in, higher on the spiritual Richter scale, so to speak. The latter could more easily be a good guess or a human intuition rather than a divine revelation.

The same can be true with the gift of healing. We once had a young woman come to our prayer meeting and get prayed with for the speedy healing of her broken leg. The next week she came back armed with dated x-rays of the leg before and after the prayer meeting. She had gone to the doctor to check on the state of her leg, been x-rayed, and been told that the rapid healing of her leg was unexplainable by medical science. On the other hand, we might pray with people who are sick, and they might report they feel better but do not seem to be completely cured. Feeling better as a result of prayer is much lower on the scale of manifest supernaturalness than coming back with evidence for an instant cure that cannot be explained by medical science.

The important point for us to recognize is that the events at the lower end of the manifest supernaturalness scale may be supernatural. God may work through someone to give an apropos prophecy that could be explained as a good guess, or he could work to make someone feel better without giving a complete healing. Those things could easily be genuine workings of God, things he did through one of his servants, even though they would not convince a skeptic that God was at work. If we believe in the power of prayer and of the gifts of the Spirit, many such events must be the special working of God.

We tend to focus on the more manifestly supernatural workings. There are various reasons for this. A conference-and-gathering orientation can contribute. If we are leading or serving at a charismatic or evangelistic conference or gathering, we want to do something that will help people turn to the Lord or grow in their faith in his power. We therefore are looking for a teaching, prophecy, or healing session in which people can come to a greater conviction that God is at work in the world. Consequently we look for manifestly supernatural stories or events, if we can find them.

An apologetic orientation can also contribute. When we are encouraging people to put their faith in God, we want to describe something that is evidence for God's being real and at work. Such concerns are natural, but they can have the unintended byproduct of getting us to see the gifts of the Spirit almost exclusively in terms of the more manifestly supernatural workings.

There is another cause that contributes to equating the operation of the gifts of the Spirit with unusual events, and that is the tendency to see strange events as supernatural. I once watched a television program in which a pastor of a charismatic church was showing a video clip of a service in which people were being prayed over and falling down afterwards ("resting in the Spirit" or "being slain in the Spirit"). He said, "Look at that! It is obviously God!"

On the other hand, the German Catholic Charismatic Renewal Theology Committee preferred to describe such events as "the falling phenomenon" because they did not seem to them obviously supernatural at all. Their position was that although such falling over might be something God produced, at other times it might be due to merely psychological causes. It especially might be due to emotionalism or be induced by heightened expectations. Whatever we might decide about the particular phenomenon at issue, seeing strange or unusual events as automatically supernatural can contribute to seeing gifts of the Spirit as unusual, not something to be found in daily life.

The gifts (and particular workings) of the Spirit operate in daily life, and they are often not very manifestly supernatural.

They might involve a "leading" to go talk to someone, getting discernment about what a child needs, praying for healing and having someone feel better, or getting some insight into Christian truth that helps in praying better or knowing how to serve God better. These seem to be more common than accurate predictions of volcanoes erupting or instantaneous healings of broken legs, but they are genuine workings of God and genuinely helpful.

Many ministry gifts, in fact, do not seem to involve any manifestly supernatural workings at all. While it is difficult to know what some of the words in the scriptural lists of gifts refer to, it seems clear that not all services they lead to involve obviously or manifestly supernatural occurrences. Nor do they all involve the kind of gift that shows up at gatherings or conferences, although many of them are "behind the scenes," making the event possible. Yet God is at work in them, as can be seen from the description of ministry gifts in 1 Peter 4:10-11: "As each has received a gift, employ it for one another, as good stewards of God's varied grace: whoever speaks, as one who utters oracles of God [literally, words from God]; whoever renders service, as one who renders it by the strength which God supplies."

First Peter seems to be assuming that some people have ministry gifts that involve speaking and others that just involve rendering service. It also seems to be saying that those who have gifts of rendering service are equipped by the strength that God supplies, strength that can be relied upon in the service. Receiving strength from God, useful as it may be, is not likely to be manifestly supernatural very often. Moreover, unless the speaking referred to is the speaking of a dramatic predictive prophecy, the speaking is not always manifestly supernatural either.

A similar point can be made by looking at Paul's description of ministry gifts in Romans 12:3-8:

> For by the grace given to me I bid every one among you not to think of himself more highly than he ought to think, but to think with sober judgment, each according to the measure of faith which God has assigned him. For as in one body we have many members, and all the members do not have the same function, so we, though many, are one body in Christ, and individually members one of another. Having gifts that differ according to the grace given to us, let us use them: if prophecy, in proportion to our faith; if service, in our serving; he who teaches, in his teaching; he who exhorts, in his exhortation; he who contributes, in liberality; he who gives aid, with zeal; he who does acts of mercy, with cheerfulness.

In this passage Paul clearly situates the individual members with ministry gifts in the whole body of the church or community. He also expects that those members can use their gifts. However all the items on the list are to be understood, the list clearly contains some items that are not manifestly supernatural, including contributing money or goods (possibly to the needy in the community) and doing acts of mercy.

Many people saw the funeral of Mother Teresa on television a few years ago. It was striking that it was on television, that so many prominent people came to it, and even more that so many secular people gave testimony to their respect for Mother Teresa and her nuns. To me it was a witness of how they could see something impressive at work in the service of these nuns, something that had a spiritual impact on them. Now, the nuns, including Mother Teresa herself, are not noted for doing manifestly supernatural things—for instance, praying for the many people they care for that they might be healed and seeing miraculous cures. What one can see in them is more of the strength that God supplies, and that itself can have an impact, even though it is not very manifestly spiritual.

I was told recently about something similar. Three people independently talked to me about a camp for children that one of our communities puts on each year. There were no reports of healings or seemingly miraculous escapes from serious injury and death. There were, in a way, no great spiritual results like conversions. While probably most if not all the children grew spiritually during the camp, it was just another step of ongoing conversion that children raised in good Christian families need to go through.

Yet all three of these people reported the camp as a powerful spiritual experience. One of them even said it was the most powerful spiritual experience she had ever had. When I asked what it was about the camp that was so powerful, the people were not able to put their finger on it, none of them. The best summary I got was something like "It was the overall experience of seeing a community of spiritual people, serving together in unity and harmony and experiencing the presence of God working in and through them." I would add that it was an experience of seeing a body with many members using different ministry gifts, none of which had manifestly supernatural expressions. That itself can reveal the Spirit of God at work.

Now, the fact that many ministry gifts do not ordinarily involve anything manifestly supernatural is a truth that can be helpful to many of us. It can at least be helpful by relieving us of the fear some have that since they have not experienced anything manifestly supernatural, God does not work through them. But it also is helpful to everyone, because the passages seem to indicate that God wants to work in all community services—even those that seem ordinary and do not seem to require any special spiritual working—because he wants to advance his kingdom through the body of Christ. All the members of the body who are serving him can therefore take advantage of his readiness to work through them.

There is another truth that can be drawn from the scriptural teaching on ministry gifts. It is true that the presence of certain ministry gifts, just like the presence of natural talents, can be a sign that someone should be chosen for a position, especially an important long-term position like minister or priest or community leader. That is, however, not a very helpful thought for those who are performing a service because someone was needed and they were willing, or at least persuadable. They may feel that they have to serve even though they have no gifts for what they are doing.

More helpful for such a situation is the thought that the Lord wants to equip those who are serving in his body. He wants to do so at least by giving us wisdom and strength for the service but also by giving, when needed, gifts like discernment and teaching, which are not manifestly supernatural, as well as by answering prayers for our service and acting through us when we serve. We can therefore seek with some confidence the ministry gift that corresponds to a service we have been given, basing our faith on the truth that God wants to work through the various members of his body to build it up—all the members.

I think we can extend this truth to being a parent. True, being a parent is natural, something a pagan can do. But if we approach our parenthood as a service within the body of Christ, a service designed to advance the kingdom of God, then we can expect spiritual gifting for it. If we have a family, God has called us to be parents, and we can expect him to work through our service as parents. Some of us may be better at it than others or may be able to serve in a more spiritually wise and powerful way. But we all can expect God to work through us when we are raising our children, and we will see more of his effectiveness if we approach the task with more spiritual confidence (expectant faith). Something similar is true for those of us who are part of celibate communities.

If, in other words, we do not approach God's gifts and graces solely in terms of particular workings of the Spirit nor focus on the more manifest ones, but if we see them as God's working through us in all Christian ministry, we will see more spiritual power and effectiveness. Whenever we have a ministry, we should look for a gift, a working of God, to accompany that ministry. The more we seek that, put our faith in that, and look for results from that, the more results we will see.

Gifts and human abilities together. We can also fail to get the benefit we should from the gifts the Spirit gives because we think of them as something God does without our cooperation. Such thinking can lead us to overlook the importance of our ability to receive certain gifts well, as those who teach about growing in the gift of healing often emphasize. It can, however, also lead us to overlook the importance of using natural skill and human effort for ministries and services, including those that make use of or are even centered on manifestly supernatural workings.

This point is perhaps best illustrated scripturally by the gift of apostleship in the early church. As we have seen, apostleship involved many of the spiritual workings described in 1 Corinthians 12:8-10. More, however, went into the service of being an apostle than just such workings. For instance, Paul said, "According to the grace of God given to me, like a skilled master builder I laid a foundation, and another man is building upon it. Let each man take care how he builds upon it" (1 Cor 3:10).

Having a ministry gift, then, means that in order to fulfill a ministry well, we need to acquire skills. We cannot rely only on having some gift. The ability to serve effectively is not just spiritually infused. God works through us, but he needs us to acquire skills if he is going to be able to get the results he is looking for. We need to become skilled builders, and we need to build with care.

In Colossians 1:28-29 Paul adds something else that went into his service as an apostle and that goes into our accomplishing whatever service we have: "Him we proclaim, warning every man and teaching every man in all wisdom, that we may present every man mature in Christ. For this I toil, striving with all the energy which he mightily inspires within me." Paul says something similar in 1 Thessalonians 2:11-12: "For you know how, like a father with his children, we exhorted each one of you and encouraged you and charged you to lead a life worthy of God, who calls you into his own kingdom and glory."

Having a Christian service, then, also involves hard work. If, for instance, like Paul we are responsible for formation, we need to meet with people, get to know them, keep up with them, admonish them, and instruct them—what we might call evangelistic follow-up or pastoral care. If we serve in the music ministry, we need to practice alone and with others, play attentively, and so on. God works in and through us, but we need to work as well, be "fellow workers" with him (1 Cor 3:9). The presence of a gift enables us to receive God's work in what we do and so be more spiritually effective, but it does not allow us to coast and just "watch what God does."

What we have talked about so far helps us to see ways in which hyperspiritualism (superspiritualism) can also be at work in the area of the gifts and graces. Hyperspiritualism can lead us to overlook the importance of human effort in mature Christian living. It can also lead us not to value (or to seriously undervalue) the "natural means" for being effective in our Christian effort, even when those means are spiritualized. It can lead us to rely only on manifestly supernatural workings and special inspirations or "leadings." We think God has to bypass us in order for something spiritual to happen.

This attitude is expressed in the following transcript from a talk that was given some years back:

> When I was coming on an airplane to the taping of these talks, I prayed as hard as I could that this wouldn't be me speaking, because if it's me speaking you're not going to get the good things that I want you to receive. You are not going to get the blessings; you are not going to get the happiness, the holiness, the power, that I would like these talks to communicate to you. For that to happen it can't be me speaking. It has to be the Holy Spirit speaking through me. And that's what Jesus promises: power, that all we have to do is open our mouths willingly, letting the Spirit speak through us.

Judging from the remainder of the talk, I think the speaker would have done better had he put more time into preparation of what he was going to say, rather than equating lack of preparation with greater reliance on the Lord.

The two most common ways hyperspiritualism in the area of service affects people now seem to be:

1. Relying heavily on the manifestly supernatural for results— for instance, "signs and wonders" as the key to evangelism— to the neglect of good explanation or diligent follow-up. For instance, some have said, "We should look for what God is doing [meaning activities where there are 'signs and wonders'] and just do that."

2. Relying on inspirations and leadings as the only way, or even the main way, to get results. In such an approach, if we rely on natural means (a good idea or, even worse, a method), we are "falling back into the flesh." For instance, some have taken the view that we should only have a community gathering "if the Spirit leads."

All this does not mean there is no room for refraining from "the natural (the human)" out of devotion to the Lord or out of a desire to act with faith. Sometimes it is fine and godly just to "live by faith" (in the common evangelical meaning of relying on God to provide finances by gifts or contributions and not using normal human financial means like getting a salary). Sometimes we need to be ready to have any ideas we come up with be shown to be inadequate. Sometimes we should refrain from action and wait for God to communicate to us how we should deal with some situation or how we should move forward to realize some goal. Sometimes we should not do anything until he acts.

Nonetheless, the natural or human is not automatically unspiritual. The more common way God works, in fact, is by spiritualizing—that is, transforming and empowering—the natural or human means of making action effective.

Some have taken the view that there is no need to be cautious in the area of spiritual gifts. There is no danger of "overdoing it," only of "underdoing it." No doubt most people are more prone to underdoing it, but there is a significant danger of overdoing it. Overdoing it can turn off people unnecessarily, but it also has the danger of making people who were once open to spiritual workings turn away because of bad experiences. The bad charismatic inhibits the good charismatic.

God with us. Ministry gifts are a blessing from God, but appreciating them can make us overlook other ways God works that could not be described in terms of ministries and gifts for those ministries. For example, he does not only work through people with a charismatic gift of healing or through people with a service of prayer for others, but he also heals people when any of us might pray for them. In other words, he answers prayer. This does not mean we will always get the results we are looking for. Nor does it mean that we are lacking in faith when results do not happen. It is like going to a doctor. Most of us have confidence that doing so will help, but we do not expect to be cured every time.

In addition, many times God just works without our asking him to do so at all. Sometimes, in fact, we only recognize that he worked when something is all over, like Abraham's servant who discovered he had found Rebecca and then recognized that God had "led him in the way" (Gn 24:27). Often, no doubt, we do not recognize what God has done on our behalf, but our lives end up going better because God is with us.

We should have "daily life expectant faith" that goes beyond our expectant faith in gifts. God is with us and wants to help us. We can expect him to do various things that are beyond our natural capability if we ask him, and often even though we do not think of asking. We should have a similar confidence in God's being with us and so trust him to be at work seeking to fulfill his purpose for our lives and for his people as a whole.

"Rod Faith"

So far we have talked about "bucket faith" and "spring faith." There is also, however, another kind of faith, "rod faith." This is the faith we need when we have a ministry gift or, at times, when we are just looking for a particular working of the Spirit. Rod faith is illustrated by Moses' experience at the crossing of the Red Sea.

Pharaoh with the whole Egyptian army had determined to pursue the people of Israel after he discovered that they were leaving the land of Egypt. When the people of Israel were at the edge of the Red Sea, they lifted up their eyes, and behold, the Egyptians were marching after them. The Israelites were in great fear. Then Moses, as their leader, had to decide what to do.

> And Moses said to the people, "Fear not, stand firm, and see the salvation of the LORD, which he will work for you today; for the Egyptians whom you see today, you shall never see again. The

LORD will fight for you, and you have only to be still."

The LORD said to Moses, "Why do you cry to me? Tell the people of Israel to go forward. Lift up your rod, and stretch out your hand over the sea and divide it, that the people of Israel may go on dry ground through the sea. And I will harden the hearts of the Egyptians so that they shall go in after them, and I will get glory over Pharaoh and all his host, his chariots, and his horsemen. And the Egyptians shall know that I am the LORD, when I have gotten glory over Pharaoh, his chariots, and his horsemen."

Then the angel of God who went before the host of Israel moved and went behind them; and the pillar of cloud moved from before them and stood behind them, coming between the host of Egypt and the host of Israel. And there was the cloud and the darkness; and the night passed without one coming near the other all night. Then Moses stretched out his hand over the sea; and the LORD drove the sea back by a strong east wind all night, and made the sea dry land, and the waters were divided. (Exodus 14:13-21)

Moses began by telling the people to stand firm—that is, not to run away. He added the Lord would fight for them. Moses then cried to God for help. He no doubt expected God to act without his having to do anything. God, however, gave him an unexpected response: "Why do you cry to me?"

If ever there seemed to be a time for bucket faith, for rescue by asking God for help without trying to do anything ourselves, this would seem to have been it. But that was not what God seemed to think. He seemed to be mainly unhappy with Moses for not having used his rod, the rod God had given him.

Moses' rod could be seen as a kind of ministry gift or equipment for ministry. He needed faith to use it. The people of Israel needed to go forward in the middle of the crisis, to act and not be passive. Certainly, they should not run away. Moses, however, also needed to act. He needed to use his rod on behalf of his people, confident that if he did, God would act as he had promised. He needed, in other words, to act with "rod faith," what people sometimes call charismatic faith.

The fourth-century church father Cyril of Jerusalem, in his *Catechetical Lectures* 5, 10-11, recognized the importance of charismatic faith and its difference from the basic faith that is belief in the truths of salvation:

> For the word faith is in the form of speech one, but has two distinct senses. For there is one kind of faith, the dogmatic, involving an assent of the soul on some particular point: and it is profitable to the soul, as the Lord said: He who hears my words, and believes him who sent me, has everlasting life, and comes not into judgment, and again, He who believes in the Son is not judged, but has passed from death unto life....
>
> But there is a second kind of faith, which is bestowed by Christ as a gift of grace. *For to one is given through the Spirit the word of wisdom, and to another the word of knowledge according to the same Spirit: to another faith, by the same Spirit, and to another gifts of healing.* This faith then, which is given by grace from the Spirit, is not merely doctrinal, but also works things above human power. *For whoever has this faith shall say to this mountain, Move over there, and it shall move.*

God gives spiritual power to us. When we rely in faith on what he has given us, we can act with greater confidence. When he gives us responsibility—a ministry or service—we can count on his power to back us. The key to doing this is not a specific act of faith or a specific prayer, although at times those are needed. It is doing what we should do, doing the actions re-quired by our service—even when those do not seem especially spiritual—confident that the Lord will work in and through our service and bring about greater results than we could by ourselves.

This power does not always mean that we can get someone healed or attain whatever we want. It does, however, mean that we can stand undefeated and see results that are more than just those that would come from good human efforts. It also means that we can be more effective in advancing the kingdom of God.

There are, then, three kinds of faith that are useful in our Christian life for receiving all the help God is willing to give:

"spring faith"— faith in the things we can definitely count on, especially in the new life God has put inside us and the ability that life gives us to grow into Christian maturity

"bucket faith"— faith that God will give us special help when we ask because we cannot do anything, or enough, to get something to happen

"rod faith"—faith that God has equipped us to do things human beings cannot accomplish on their own.

There is, in addition, one other kind of faith that we might easily overlook: faith that the "Lord of hosts is with us" (Ps 46:7), even when we do not recognize our need for any particular help from him.

We need all these kinds of faith.

God's action does not necessarily depend on our exercising the right kind of faith or even any faith at all. He is at work to accomplish his purposes and is not limited by our weaknesses. Nonetheless, he is encouraging us to grow in faith, and if we do, we will be more effective servants in the cause of his kingdom.

THIS GIVES US OUR FOURTH CONCLUSION:

Our charismatic spirituality is based on the conviction that God acts in our world to make Christians effective in their service of him, without implying that (spiritualized) natural means are worthless or unimportant.

CHAPTER FIVE

Worship in Spirit and Truth

If we are spiritual people who want a charismatic spirituality, we will approach various areas of the Christian life in "a charismatic way." Worship is one of them. To be sure, worship is only one area affected by being charismatic. We could also, for example, speak about evangelism and how it could work more effectively as a result of a charismatic orientation. However, worship is central to the charismatic experience, for reasons considered below.

Responding to the work of the Holy Spirit is only one aspect of our communion with God and our corporate and individual prayer life. Other things also go into relating well with God, like listening to or reading Scripture. This chapter does not contain a full treatment of Christian worship and prayer. Nor is it a chapter on how to have a good prayer time or lead a good prayer meeting. Rather, it considers the foundation of good prayer: the work of the Holy Spirit in making it possible for us to worship well.

New Covenant Worship: In or by the Holy Spirit

The Holy Spirit makes possible the new covenant relationship with God. His role is commonly designated in Scripture by a phrase that can be translated "in the Holy Spirit" or "by the Holy Spirit," depending on the context. There is a Greek word [en] in that phrase that can be translated "in" or "by." Like our word "in," it indicates a spatial location, but it is also used to indicate agency and then can be translated "by." Scripture tells us that many things happen in or by the Holy Spirit and that we are to do many things in or by the Holy Spirit. If, then, we understand the phrase better, we will understand better how to respond to the work of the Holy Spirit, including his work in Christian worship.

The role of the Holy Spirit in worship is spoken about in the passage in John 4 about Jesus and the woman at the well, which we have already considered. As we have seen, Jesus first spoke to the woman about the gift of God, the fountain of living water that he would put inside those who turned to him. The conversation then, in verse 19, turned to worship:

> The woman said to him, "Sir, I perceive that you are a prophet. Our fathers worshiped on [en] this mountain; and you say that in [en] Jerusalem is the place where men ought to worship."
>
> Jesus said to her, "Woman, believe me, the hour is coming when neither on this mountain nor in Jerusalem will you worship the Father. You worship what you do not know; we worship what we know, for salvation is from the Jews. But the hour is coming, and now is, when the true worshipers will worship the Father in [en] spirit and truth, for such the Father seeks to worship him. God is spirit, and those who worship him must worship in spirit and truth."
>
> The woman said to him, "I know that Messiah is coming (he who is called Christ); when he comes, he will show us all things."
>
> Jesus said to her, "I who speak to you am he." (John 4:19-26)

Note, first of all, that the same word is used in Greek for "in" and "on." (The three places it is used are marked on the text above.) The repeated use of this word means that Mount Gerizim, Jerusalem, and the Holy Spirit ["spirit and truth"] are spoken about as parallel to one another and so are being compared with one another.

The Samaritan woman spoke about "this mountain," possibly pointing to Mount Gerizim, which was right above the place where they were conversing. *This mountain* and *in Jerusalem* refer to places of worship, places where there were temples, although the temple on Mount Gerizim was in ruins at the time. The temple on Mount Gerizim was the Samaritan place of worship, and of course the temple at Jerusalem, built on Mount Zion, was the Jewish place of worship. These were places where the respective groups believed God could be "met" or contacted and where offerings would be accepted and prayer heard.

In an attempt to say that she did not have to be concerned with Jesus because she was Samaritan and Samaritan worship was different than his, the woman contrasted Mount Gerizim and Jerusalem. Jesus, in response, replied that this difference no longer had the same importance as previously, because both Mount Gerizim and Jerusalem were even at that moment being replaced. He used an unusual phrase, "the hour is coming and now is," to indicate that a change would be happening in the near future. He was speaking of the "hour" of his crucifixion and resurrection, as we now know. But even at the moment he was speaking to the Samaritan woman, that hour was starting, because the new covenant was beginning by his ministry and would be definitively established shortly.

He then spoke about what would replace Mount Gerizim and Jerusalem. "True worshippers will worship in spirit and truth." *Spirit and truth* may be interpreted as "the Spirit of truth" or "the Spirit and the truth [which Christ teaches and brings]." Either way, the phrase includes a reference to the Holy Spirit, so Jesus is speaking of worship in or by the Holy Spirit.

The Holy Spirit, then, is a "place" or means of contact with

God. He has replaced the physical temple(s) central to old covenant worship. New covenant people do not need to go to a physical location to make contact with God and worship him in the way he wants. We can make contact with him by means of the Holy Spirit, the gift of God within us.

Likely, therefore, the Holy Spirit is understood to be something like a medium or means of communication, as a physical place can be the means of putting people into communication with one another or, in old covenant understanding, with God. To use an example, when we want to get across the Atlantic, we can go "by" air or water. Air and water are media that can enable us to make connection. We are in them and therefore move by them. In an analogous way, when we worship "in or by the Spirit," the Holy Spirit makes a connection between the Father and us.

Or to use a different example, the Holy Spirit is like the airwaves that allow us to make radio contact with someone in a distant spot. In the Holy Spirit's case, he allows us to make contact with God, to come into the heavenly presence of God so that we can make connection with him in a way we could not have otherwise. Put in a more Trinitarian way, the Holy Spirit enters into us, dwells in us, and so enables us to come into the presence of God the Father, because he himself is one with the Father and always with him.

There are two other passages in the New Testament that speak about the role of the Holy Spirit in worship in a way that develops what was said in John. The first is in Ephesians 2:17-18: "And he came and preached peace to you who were far off and peace to those who were near; for through him we both have access in one Spirit to the Father."

The second is in Revelation 4:1-2: "After this I looked, and lo, in heaven an open door! And the first voice, which I had heard speaking to me like a trumpet, said, 'Come up hither, and I will show you what must take place after this.' At once I was in the Spirit, and lo, a throne stood in heaven, with one seated on the throne!

Access in Ephesians 2:18 is a ceremonial word. It was used to speak of the way a priest could approach God's presence in the Holy of Holies in the temple. Most Israelites could only come as far as the Court of the Israelites, in front of the temple building. Priests, however, could enter the building itself when they were offering incense. The high priest could even enter the Holy of Holies itself once a year. These differences in ability to approach God were sometimes spoken about as degrees of "access" to God's presence, with the high priest having the greatest access of all.

According to Ephesians 2:18, the blessing of the new covenant means that both Gentile Christians, "those who were far off," and Jewish Christians, "those who were near," can have direct *access to the Father*. We can come more immediately into his presence than old covenant people could. And we can do this *in one Spirit* because the Holy Spirit in us is a means of contact with the Father.

What Ephesians describes in theological terms, Revelation describes in narrative terms. John, in chapter 4, received a vision. He saw an open door in the sky, and a voice invited him to come to heaven, the place of God's presence. He then was "in the Spirit," and as a result he found himself in heaven, having been given access to God's throne. The Spirit, in other words, put him into the presence of God in heaven.

John saw in a vision what happens to all new covenant people, even though we cannot see it with our eyes. In the phrase of Ephesians, we can have "access to the Father"—that is, we can come into his presence. In his fifth sermon on the nativity of the Lord, Leo the Great said, "If we are indeed the temple of God and if the Spirit of God lives in us, then what every believer has within himself is greater than what he admires in the skies." C.S. Lewis, in the *Chronicles of Narnia*, gives a picture of this with a wardrobe, a piece of furniture for hanging up coats and similar pieces of clothing. The children in the story go into the wardrobe and find a world inside, Narnia, that is much greater than the wardrobe itself.

In a similar way, we can "enter into ourselves" and find there a world much greater than ourselves, heaven itself. We can "turn to the Lord" and find ourselves standing in his presence. We might describe this as heaven's coming down into us or as our going up to heaven. Both descriptions are true at the same time, because we are talking about a change of relationship with God that changes our ability to make contact with him. That change is produced by the Holy Spirit's coming to dwell in us.

This all raises a question. We know that God is everywhere—"omnipresent," to use the technical term. In what new way, then, does the Holy Spirit put us into God's presence?

The answer to that question comes from what we have already said. God is always with us and always sees us, but he does not always make it possible for people to turn to him and make contact with him. Those who are "living in sin" are shut off from him and at best can send off an appeal to him, like sending a letter to a distant shore. Old covenant people could pray to him, but the fullness of interaction, "meeting God," could only happen in certain places—in fact, in only one place once the temple in Jerusalem was built. New covenant people, however, can "come into his presence" whenever they wish to turn to him. The door is open, so to speak. As a result, new covenant people can turn to the Lord and enter his presence in prayer, confident of making contact with him.

There is something else that the Holy Spirit does when he

comes to us that is also important to worship. This is described in Galatians 4:4-7:

> But when the time had fully come, God sent forth his Son, born of woman, born under the law, to redeem those who were under the law, so that we might receive adoption as sons. And because you are sons, God has sent the Spirit of his Son into our hearts, crying, "Abba! Father!" So through God you are no longer a slave but a son, and if a son then an heir.

When the Holy Spirit comes into our hearts, he does not just put us into contact with God; he also changes us so that we can interact with God. He does this by giving us a new relationship to God, "adoption as sons," a relationship that involves a new aptitude for relating to God. As a result, we can receive and know how to respond to the impulse or inspiration of the Holy Spirit that moves us to address God as Father.

If the work of the Holy Spirit is analogous to the way telephone wires or the electric impulses traveling through those telephone wires allow our computers to make contact with people far away, it is also like the installation of an internet access program. Without such a program, no matter how good the connection, we could not communicate. Something has to be changed on our side, in our computer. It needs to be programmed so it can receive certain communications. In an analogous way, we need to be changed inside so that we can respond as sons and daughters of God once we come into God's presence. This the Holy Spirit does.

The Holy Spirit, then, makes worship—new covenant worship, spiritual worship—possible. He does that by making a very fundamental change in how we can relate to God. In order to make such a change in an ongoing way, he has to dwell inside us. His indwelling presence in us, then, makes new covenant worship possible.

The connection between the presence of the Holy Spirit in us and new covenant worship can also be seen in the scriptural accounts of what happened when the Holy Spirit was given. There are three main passages in which the coming of the Holy Spirit on new Christians is described with enough fullness to show how people recognized someone had received the Holy Spirit. The first we already considered in the first chapter of this book, the description of the outpouring of the Holy Spirit on the Day of Pentecost: "And there appeared to them tongues as of fire, distributed and resting on each one of them. And they were all filled with the Holy Spirit and began to speak in other tongues, as the Spirit gave them utterance" (Acts 2:3-4).

The second is Acts 10:44-48, the description of the outpouring of the Holy Spirit on the first group of Gentile believers:

> While Peter was still saying this, the Holy Spirit fell on all who heard the word. And the believers from among the circumcised who came with Peter were amazed, because the gift of the Holy Spirit had been poured out even on the Gentiles. For they heard them speaking in tongues and extolling God. Then Peter declared, "Can any one forbid water for baptizing these people who have received the Holy Spirit just as we have?" And he commanded them to be baptized in the name of Jesus Christ. Then they asked him to remain for some days.

The third is Acts 19:1-7, the description of a group of disciples of John the Baptist who become disciples of Christ:

> While Apollos was at Corinth, Paul passed through the upper country and came to Ephesus. There he found some disciples. And he said to them, "Did you receive the Holy Spirit when you believed?" And they said, "No, we have never even heard that there is a Holy Spirit." And he said, "Into what then were you baptized?" They said, "Into John's baptism." And Paul said, "John baptized with the baptism of repentance, telling the

people to believe in the one who was to come after him, that is, Jesus." On hearing this, they were baptized in the name of the Lord Jesus. And when Paul had laid his hands upon them, the Holy Spirit came on them; and they spoke with tongues and prophesied. There were about twelve of them in all.

If we look at these passages, we see that three things are mentioned: tongues, prophecy, and extolling God. In other words, when the Holy Spirit came on people for the first time, they began to pray in tongues, prophesy, or extol God. Those watching them saw a change happen, and one sign of that change was that they were inspired to praise God, since speaking in tongues, prophecy, and extolling God were probably all ways of praising God.

When the people spoke in tongues they were praying. We can see this fact by the way Paul spoke about tongues in 1 Corinthians 14. He said, "For one who speaks in a tongue speaks not to men but to God; for no one understands him, but he utters mysteries in the Spirit" (v. 2), and, "If I pray in a tongue, my spirit prays but my mind is unfruitful" (v. 14). Moreover, in Acts 2:11, the onlookers described what they were hearing by saying, "We hear them telling in our own tongues the mighty works of God." Likely this means they were praising God.

Prophecy can also be prayer, as we can see from Luke 1:67: "And his father Zechariah was filled with the Holy Spirit and prophesied, saying, 'Blessed be the Lord God of Israel, for he has visited and redeemed his people.'" That means that when the disciples at Ephesus were baptized in the Spirit, they probably were also praising God, since the prophesying that happened, like their speaking in tongues, was an initial response to the presence of the Holy Spirit in them and did not seem to be directed to Paul or anyone else who might have been with him. And of course, extolling God is just another way of saying "praising God."

The initial indication of the gift of the Spirit, then, seems to be inspired praise. Those who have been baptized in the Spirit begin to praise God. This is the "natural" (spiritually natural) response to being put into experiential contact with God. Worship and an ability and desire to worship, therefore, is a sign of being baptized in the Spirit. The Holy Spirit installs, so to speak, "the worship program" into us so that we can worship in a way we could not before. In addition, he begins to inspire (work in) us to use it. This is an indication that worship is central to the work of the Holy Spirit.

The worship of God that the Holy Spirit brings about is not only individual but corporate worship as well. We have already seen that the Holy Spirit does not work just in individuals separately but also unites people into something corporate, one body. We already considered the section of Ephesians 2:20-22, where it speaks about "Christ Jesus himself being the cornerstone, in whom the whole structure is joined together and grows into a holy temple in the Lord; in whom you also are built into it for a dwelling place of God in the Spirit." The result of his unifying men and women in Christ includes unifying them in worship, because that is what we do in "a holy temple."

We also can see that the Holy Spirit creates a unity in worship by putting together again a passage from Paul, which speaks theologically, with a passage in Revelation, which presents the same truth in narrative form. The first is Romans 15:5-6:

> May the God of steadfastness and encouragement grant you to
> live in such harmony with one another, in accord with Christ

Jesus, that together you may with one voice glorify the God and Father of our Lord Jesus Christ.

The second is Revelation 14:1-5:

> Then I looked, and lo, on Mount Zion stood the Lamb, and with him a hundred and forty-four thousand who had his name and his Father's name written on their foreheads. And I heard a voice from heaven like the sound of many waters and like the sound of loud thunder; the voice I heard was like the sound of harpers playing on their harps, and they sing a new song before the throne and before the four living creatures and before the elders. No one could learn that song except the hundred and forty-four thousand who had been redeemed from the earth. It is these who have not defiled themselves with women, for they are chaste; it is these who follow the Lamb wherever he goes; these have been redeemed from mankind as first fruits for God and the Lamb, and in their mouth no lie was found, for they are spotless.

Paul tells us that the Holy Spirit unites us so that we can worship God together with one voice. The same Spirit is in all of us, and he therefore gives us all the same orientation. When he makes us be "in accord with Christ Jesus," in tune with him, we are in "harmony with one another." The result is, or at least can be, unified worship.

Revelation provides a picture of this in operation. The Lamb is standing on Mount Zion, the place of the temple, and the 144,000 are with him. These are the disciples of the Lord, those who belong to him. The number seems to indicate that they are the new covenant people of God. They worship God together, singing one "new song." They are able to do that because they can hear the worship in heaven, and what they hear there they reproduce on earth.

I once had an experience that illustrates this. I was in a car with someone and the radio was on. We stopped at a red light, and I looked over at the next car to see the driver beating time to music. It was in perfect time with the music we were listening to. I realized that he must be listening to the same radio program we were. Something similar should happen with a body of Christians. They should be like the disciples of the Lamb, "listening to" the same heavenly music and joining in on earth.

Spiritual, Charismatic Worship

If the work of the Holy Spirit produces worship in us, we then have the question of when our worship is spiritual or spiritualized. What criterion can we use to determine this?

This is similar to the question, "When is our driving spiritual?" A caricature of a charismatic response might say, The sign that our driving is spiritual is that we find a parking place when we pray for it. That is, however, not an adequate answer.

The first answer is provided in Romans 8:9. There the apostle Paul is talking about the difference the Holy Spirit makes in redeemed people: "But you are not in the flesh, you are in the Spirit, if in fact the Spirit of God dwells in you. Any one who does not have the Spirit of Christ does not belong to him." Our driving or our worship or anything we do is spiritual, first of all, when the Holy Spirit dwells in us. But there is more to it.

We find a further answer in Galatians 5:16-23, the passage on the fruit of the Spirit. To summarize what was said in chapter 2, our driving is spiritual when we are spiritualized, that is, when the Holy Spirit is in us, but also when we drive in a spiritualized way. This means we have to drive in the fruit of the Spirit, keeping the commandments of God and manifesting the character of God when we drive. The same thing is true of our worship. We have to worship in the fruit of the Spirit, keeping the commandments of God.

Galatians 5:16-23, the passage on the fruits of the Spirit, teaches about the opposite of spiritual worship, the "works of the flesh" that could keep our worship from being spiritualized: idolatry and sorcery (divination). We could add superstition, spiritualism, and other similar practices of worship condemned by the Scripture. When these are present, our worship is not spiritualized.

Sometimes Christians think that any worship is good because it shows an interest in God and spiritual things. That view, however, is diametrically opposed to the teaching of the Scripture, which condemns false worship very strongly. Our worship is only spiritual when we are not idolaters, when we have true belief (including belief in the Incarnation and the Trinity), when we do not engage in spiritualism or divination, when we do not engage in human sacrifice, as some pagans did, and so on—and when we have the Holy Spirit dwelling in us so that we can relate to God as his sons and daughters.

Most formal Christian worship, then, is spiritual because it is done by people in whom the Holy Spirit dwells and is done in a godly, orthodox way. The church service this week, formal as it may be and lacking in vitality as it may be, is probably spiritual. To be sure, this may not be true of some church services that are identified as Christian. They may be highly secularized or influenced by Eastern religions or New Age thought. But it is true of a large number of them, including those that do not impress us much with their vitality.

A third answer can be found in 1 Corinthians 14. In verse 12 Paul says, "Since you are eager for manifestations of the Spirit, strive to excel in building up the church," and in verse 40 he says, "All things should be done decently and in order." The third criterion, then, is that worship should be done in a way that builds up the body of Christ and so is done decently and in order. This is actually an expression of the fruit of the

Spirit, although it is helpful to mention it separately. Love leads us to seek the good of others and of the body. It means, at times, giving up our preferences for the good of the body, including our spiritual preferences.

This has implications for those of us who would like to see our church services more spiritually vital. When we attend church, we should enter into the service as we find it, at least if it is orthodox and does not violate the commandments. That does not mean that we cannot propose improvements when appropriate. But it does mean that we need to participate in the service as it is.

This leads us to another question: When is our worship *charismatic*? There are three answers that have been commonly given. The first is that our worship is charismatic when it is done in "charismatic style." By that people seem to mean the style characteristic of the charismatic movement.

Worship in the charismatic style tends to be spontaneous or unstructured, as distinguished from more formal worship using set words and sequences. It also includes special practices, such as the raising of hands and the "word of prayer" (everyone praying softly out loud at the same time). It usually has lively music, often accompanied by participants' movement in time to the beat. It almost always has active, expressive participation by those present, including chances for anyone to "share" or contribute. Several people are usually involved in leading a charismatic activity. The charismatic style can be helpful, but it is not enough to make our worship charismatic.

The second answer commonly given is that worship is charismatic when it is open to spiritual gifts or inspirations for worship. Several passages in the New Testament give us examples of such worship. The first is 1 Corinthians 14:26-33, where Paul instructs the Corinthians how to have an orderly service.

> What then, brethren? When you come together, each one has a hymn, a lesson, a revelation, a tongue, or an interpretation. Let all things be done for edification. If any speak in a tongue, let there be only two or at most three, and each in turn; and let one interpret. But if there is no one to interpret, let each of them keep silence in church and speak to himself and to God. Let two or three prophets speak, and let the others weigh what is said. If a revelation is made to another sitting by, let the first be silent. For you can all prophesy one by one, so that all may learn and all be encouraged; and the spirits of prophets are subject to prophets. For God is not a God of confusion but of peace.

The second is Colossians 3:16-17:

> Let the word of Christ dwell in you richly, teach and admonish one another in all wisdom, and sing psalms and hymns and spiritual songs with thankfulness in your hearts to God. And whatever you do, in word or deed, do everything in the name of the Lord Jesus, giving thanks to God the Father through him.

The third is Ephesians 5:18-20:

> And do not get drunk with wine, for that is debauchery; but be filled with the Spirit, addressing one another in psalms and hymns and spiritual songs, singing and making melody to the Lord with all your heart, always and for everything giving thanks in the name of our Lord Jesus Christ to God the Father.

All three passages point to services where many people can contribute if they think they have something to offer. The first clearly speaks about the presence of spiritual gifts, and the other two likely do as well, because they are probably describing inspired contributions to worship.

Charismatic worship, then, is worship in which spiritual gifts give rise to various contributions, including tongues, prophecy, and inspired prayers and songs. As the above passages indicate, there seems to be some connection between a worship service that has time open for everyone to contribute and one in which spiritual gifts are used. For fully charismatic worship there needs to be some space for active, informal participation.

The word *fully* in the previous sentence is important. I do not want to say that non-Pentecostal, noncharismatic church services are not charismatic at all. Very often the preacher or homilist at a normal church service or a music leader contributes in ways that we can experience as having charismatic power. But the rest of the congregation has no opportunity (or, usually, inclination) to contribute, regardless of what God maybe doing in them.

The phrase *some space* is likewise intentional. I do not want to say that everything has to be informal or open in order to have charismatic worship. Informal and formal worship can be combined and often are better than either by itself. In fact, there is nothing so dead as a dead spontaneous prayer meeting. The formal patterns can foster active worship and can be especially helpful when those present do not seem to have much to contribute. In fact, most Pentecostal and charismatic groups, no matter how much emphasis they put on open, spontaneous meetings, seem to have a certain pattern to their worship, often relying on music that is led and prepared talks.

Nonetheless, for fully charismatic worship, there needs to be some open space. That is the reason why there seems to be some equation between informality or spontaneity and charismatic worship. The informality, however, is not the key factor. The presence of spiritual or charismatic gifts is.

The third answer to the question of when worship is charismatic is when the people present, or the core of them, have an experiential relationship with God. According to this answer, charismatic worship is worship by people who have been baptized in the Spirit. This is something that cannot easily be identified by external signs but can often be "felt" intuitively. When a group of people has an experiential contact with the Lord, when they turn to him with expectant faith, some spiritual interaction seems to happen that is absent in many other situations. And the Lord seems to interact with such a group, both in regard to what he does for them individually and the way he leads them corporately.

It is the experiential relationship with the Lord that brings "the charismatic emphasis" of praise and worship. When people have experienced the Lord and know his greatness and majesty in a personal way, they desire to praise and worship the Lord. In addition, they tend to pray in faith for the things they need, since they have conviction that he is there and that he answers prayer.

Again, we need to be careful in emphasizing the experiential nature of people's relationship with God. Having an experiential relationship with him and expressing that in prayer is not the same as having "devotional feelings." Many, in fact, focus on trying to stir up their feelings of devotion, or they evaluate their prayer by how intensely or fervently they felt during it. When, however, God is real to us, someone we know, and our relationship with him is interactive, our worship is experiential, even if we are not experiencing much in the way of devotional feelings. This goes back to what we discussed in the second chapter about an experiential relationship with God.

Speaking in tongues provides us with an object lesson of how we can worship in a spiritual way without devotional feelings. This gift is often somewhat routine. Many times we even do not notice that we are praying in tongues. It can be like breathing in this respect. It most commonly is not exciting or moving. It is, however, usually prayer, and we know it is.

If we equate devotional feelings with an experiential relationship with God, we are often derailed by "dryness" in prayer. Sometimes the dryness comes because of sickness or other circumstances in life, usually trying ones. Sometimes it comes when we are entering a new stage of life or a new stage of the spiritual life. Periods of dryness often lead to the temptation to stop praying because it is no longer satisfying. This in itself can be helpful in our spiritual growth. The dryness forces us to choose God over a satisfying experience of prayer, with the result that it helps purify our motivation for prayer. We pray because we want a good relationship with God, not because we want a good spiritual experience.

In addition, different people respond to the emotional or feeling aspect of life in different ways. Older people respond differently than younger people. Men respond differently than women. Personality types respond in various ways. Some of us find devotional feelings easier to have than others. Some find that they once experienced many and strong devotional feelings but do so less now that they are older or their circumstances in life have changed. The variation in devotional feeling is not a reliable sign of whether our prayer life is good.

This leads us to still another question. Our worship is spiritual when we are spiritualized in the way we pray. Our worship is charismatic either when we are open to spiritual or charismatic gifts in worship or when we have an experiential relationship with God or both. But when is our worship good? Or to ask the question another way, What is the criterion for success in prayer and worship?

We have to begin by asking why we pray. The answer should not be "to have a good experience." The answer should not be to benefit ourselves, to get something out of our relationship with God, or to get him to help us—important as such things may be. The answer should be to be in a good relationship with God and to relate to him well. We should relate to God for his own sake, out of love of him, not just for what we get out of the relationship. Our prayer and worship, individually and corporately, then, should be an expression of our relationship with God and should be motivated by a desire to have a good relationship with him.

The most important things we need to do to relate to God well, of course, are to have faith in him and obey him, to love him with our whole mind, soul, heart and strength. But when we pray, we turn to him in a conscious, personal way. We address ourselves to him, while at the same time expressing our intention by posture, gesture and so forth. We do that because our relationship with God is personal and therefore has to involve personal interaction. However, it has to involve a special kind of personal interaction, because he is God, our Creator and Lord, the infinite, eternal source of all that we are and will be.

In order to relate to God as God, we need to honor him or glorify him. We honor him especially by praise and worship. We need to acknowledge who God is and our acceptance of that, our appreciation of that. We also need to thank him. We need to thank him not just for the things we are currently grateful for or happy about but for everything he has done for us to create us and sustain us. We need to do so because he is the source of all good and because every moment of our existence we are benefiting from his goodness to us.

We also need to hear God—hear his Word, hear what he has to say to us. We need to read his Word in Scripture and listen for it in prayer. We need to hear him because his Word is life, because we live by knowing the truth he teaches, and because doing his will is our delight. We need to repent for our sins as needed—confessing them, rejecting them, making up for the damage we have done when we can. We need to ask him for the things we need, both the things we need every day and the things we are immediately in need of.

In other words, in order to have a good relationship with God, we need to interact with him in a personal way. This is somewhat like the way we relate to other human beings but also somewhat different—because he is God. If we do those things in prayer that we need to do to have a good relationship with him, our personal prayer life and our community worship are good.

We might add that there are charismatic emphases that can be present in good worship. Those who have had a charismatic experience will probably emphasize praise and worship more than others. They will also seek to have God speak, not just in the general way he speaks to those who read his Word but also in a way relevant to their current situation in life. They may also look for inspirations for their personal prayer time, as they do for prayer meetings.

Such charismatic emphases are helpful in worship and can improve prayer. But prayer and worship can be good without them as long as it is a means of expressing and maintaining a good relationship with God.

There can be more. We can have "visions and revelations" and be "caught up to the third heaven" (2 Cor 12:1-2). We can have a special gift for prayer. We can immerse ourselves in Scripture, gaining "wisdom and understanding, counsel and might,... knowledge and the fear of the Lord" (Is 11:2). We can "continue in supplications and prayers day and night" (1 Tm 5:5). Nonetheless, our prayer life is good if we do the basic things needed to have a good relationship with God. We should not only notice what more there could be and fail to notice when we have a good relationship with God. A life of prayer and worship that is pleasing to God is accessible to all of us, no matter how busy we may be or how weak we may be.

THIS GIVES US OUR FIFTH CONCLUSION:

Charismatic spirituality involves approaching a particular area of the Christian life, like prayer and worship or evangelism, in a charismatic way, by expecting the Holy Spirit to make direct, experiential contact for us with God so that we might receive personal spiritual strengthening and added light and power, including gifts and graces, to act effectively in that area.

God's Purpose for Charismatic Spirituality

The Lord poured out his Spirit for a purpose, as we saw in the first two chapters. He had something he was aiming at, both for the human race as a whole and for individuals in the human race. His Spirit was given so that he might enter into the life of the Christian people as a whole, including each grouping of Christians, and into the life of individual Christians and bring them to the purpose for which he created the human race. The New Testament and all good Christian teaching tell us that we cannot live the new covenant life by ourselves; God needs to work in us and through us. In fact, he will "equip" [us] with everything good that [we] may do his will, working in [us] that which is pleasing in his sight, through Jesus Christ, to whom be glory for ever and ever. Amen" (Heb 13:21).

The purpose of having a charismatic spirituality, then, is not to create a special group of Christians but to experience the work of the Holy Spirit in our lives the way God intended for all Christians when he poured out his Spirit on the Day of

Pentecost on Mount Zion. Good charismatic spirituality is achieved in our prayer life and in our life as a whole when we love God and neighbor by the power of the Holy Spirit. It is a spirituality of renewal of the Christian basics, not a special spirituality, a special way only for those who might find it helpful.

Certainly there are many features of the charismatic movement in our day that constitute "a special way," features that many have found helpful but that are not integral to full Christianity. But what we have talked about in this book as charismatic spirituality is for all. We can enter into it by faith in what Christian revelation teaches that God wishes to do for those who receive his Son as their Lord and Savior.

Charismatic spirituality does involve some special emphases nowadays. There is a special emphasis on experience, although it should not make us experience-focused. There is a special emphasis on faith, although it should not make us neglect love of God and love of neighbor. These are special emphases that come from a call to renewal addressed to cultural Christians or traditional Christians who lack spiritual vitality. It is also a call addressed to good traditional Christians who have spiritual vitality but who lack the power of the Holy Spirit, which could make them effective in advancing his kingdom.

These emphases may come from a special call to Christians in our age due to the transition of the Christian people from a Christendom situation to a diaspora situation, one in which they cannot rely on the societal supports but need more of a direct spiritual support from the Lord. Be that as it may, the special emphases in a charismatic spirituality for today are emphases of elements integral to Christianity. The work of the Holy Spirit is not an optional extra, much less a specialty item.

In order to be helpful, however, a charismatic spirituality needs to be a mature Christian spirituality. It needs to sustain a relational faithfulness to God and others. It needs to carry us through trials, dryness, routine, temptation and aging. It needs to be a balanced spirituality. It cannot be hyperspiritual, constantly leaving our humanity behind or ignoring it rather than seeking to convert and transform it, to spiritualize it. It cannot just live by "charismatic novelties"—new waves, rediscovery of spiritual gifts and healings, new and deeper experiences—although such things can be helpful at times.

The basis of a mature, faithful, balanced charismatic spirituality is the conviction that we have the Holy Spirit—a spring of living water, a dynamo of spiritual power—inside. Such a conviction needs to be more than notional. It needs to be a confident faith that allows us to draw upon the Holy Spirit for our everyday Christian discipleship. The sign of its presence is the "joy inspired by the Holy Spirit" (1 Thes 1:6), manifested in the desire given by the Spirit, even in the midst of tribulation, to praise and thank God, to give him glory.

APPENDIX

The Work of the Holy Spirit in Scripture

This section contains lists of passages that explicitly mention the Holy Spirit and teach about his work in us. The passages are grouped by topic, using the conceptuality followed in this book, and are intended to be useful for a follow-up study. They also provide a more extensive summary of the scriptural basis for the presentation in this book.

THE OLD TESTAMENT

The prophecies of the outpouring of the Spirit:
Is 32:14-20; 44:1-5; 59:19-21; Ez 36:22-36 [Jer 31:31-34; 11:17-21; 18:30-32]; 37:1-14; Jl 2:28-32 (3:1-5).

Prophecies of Christ being filled with the Spirit:
Is 11:1-5, 42:1-9; 61:1-3.

Examples of charismatic (ministry) gifts: Gn 41:37-40;
Ex 28:1-4; 31:1-11; 35:30-35; Nm 11:10-30; Nm 27:15-23;
Dt 34:9; 1 Sm 10:1-13; 16:6-13, 14-23; 2 Kgs 2:9-15; Neh 9:30-31; Mi 3:5-8; Zec 7:12; and probably Neh 9:18-21; Is 28:5-6; 63:10-14; Dn 4:8-9, 18; 5:11-12, 14; 6:3; Hos 9:7; Zec 4:6-10; and possibly Ps 51:10-11.

**Examples of particular workings of the Spirit (spiritual
gifts):** Nm 24:1-4; Jgs 3:7-11; 6:33-35; 11:28-33; 14:5-6, 19;
15:14-17; 1 Sm 11:5-8; 19:18-24; 2 Sm 23:1-4; 1 Kgs 18:12;
22:19-28 [2 Chr 18:18-27]; 2 Kgs 3:13-20; 1 Chr 12:16-18;
2 Chr 15:1-2; 20:13-17; 24:20-21; Ez 2:1-3; 3:10-15, 22-24;
8:1-4; 11:1-6, 22-25; 43:1-5.

**Some significant deuterocanonical/apocryphal passages on
the work of the Holy Spirit:** Wis 7-9, especially 9:17-18; and
possibly Sir 39:1-11; 48:22-25.

THE NEW TESTAMENT

The baptism and ministry of Jesus: Mt 3:13-17 (Mk 1:9-11;
Lk 3:21-22); Jn 1:31-34; Acts 10:36-38; Mt 4:1 (Mk 1:12-13;
Lk 4:1-2); Lk 4:1-2, 14-15, 16-22; 10:21-22: Mt 12:15-21, 27-
28; (see Lk 11:19-20); and probably Jn 3:31-36; 6:63-64.
In addition, passages about the birth of Christ: Mt 1:18-25;
Lk 1:34-35; and passages about the resurrection/ glorification
of Christ: Rom 1:1-6; 1 Cor 15:42-50; 1 Tm 3:16; and possibly
Heb 9:13-14; 1 Pt 3:18-19.

The gift of the Spirit resulting in his indwelling in us:

Descriptions of the outpouring of the Spirit: Acts 2; 8:14-24;
9:10-19; 10:1-11:18 (Acts 15:6-11); 19:1-7; and possibly
Jn 20:19-25.

References to the gift of the Spirit: Mt 3:11-12 (Mk 1:7-8;
Lk 3:16-13; Jn 1:29-34); Lk 11:13; Jn 3:5-8; 4:7-15; 14:15-17;
24:49; Acts 1:4-5, 8; 5:32; Rom 5:5; 7:5-6; 8:9-11, 14-17, 23;
15:15-16; 1 Cor 2:12; 3:16-17; 6:11, 19-20; 12:12-13;
2 Cor 1:21-22; 3:1-6; 5:5; 11:4; Gal 3:1-5, 13-14; 4:4-7; 5:4-6,
25; Eph 1:13-14; 4:30; 5:18-20; 1 Thes 4:8; Ti 3:4-7; Heb 6:1-5;
1 Jn 3:24; 4:13; 10:28-29; 1 Pt 1:1-2; Jude 19; and probably
2 Cor 13:14; 17-18; 2 Thes 2:13; Jas 4:4-5; 1 Jn 5:6-8; Rv 22:17;
and possibly Jn 14:15-17; 25-27; 15:26-27; 16:7-11; 1 Pt 4:14.

The experience of the Spirit: Jn 14:15-17; Rom 8:14-17; Gal 3:1-5; 4:4-7; Eph 5:18-20; 1 Jn 3:24; 4:13; and probably Rom 8:23, 26-27; Heb 6:1-4.

The fruit of the Spirit: Rom 8:1-17; 14:17; 15:13; 1 Cor 3:1-4; Gal 5:4-6, 13-26; 6:1, 8; Eph 4:30; 5:18-20; and possibly Rom 5:5.

The seven gifts: [Is 11:1-5; Ps 143:10]; Acts 6:1-6; 11:22-24; 15:28-29; 19:21; Rom 9:1-2; Rom 12:11; 1 Cor 2:6-16; Eph 1:15-23; 3:14-19; Col 1:9-14; and probably 1 Cor 2:12; Gal 6:1; Phil 1:19-20; 1 Thes 1:6-7; 2 Tm 1:6; 1 Jn 2:18-27.

The temple of the Holy Spirit: Jn 4:21-26; 1 Cor 3:1-9; 3:16-17; 6:19-20; 1 Pt 2:4-5.

Worship in the Holy Spirit: Jn 4:21-26; Acts 2:3-4; 10:44-48; 19:4-7; Rom 8:14-17; 1 Cor 3:1-9, 16-17, 6:19-20; 14:1-5, 13-19, 26-31; 2 Cor 3:1-6, 14-16; Gal 4:4-7; Eph 6:18; Phil 3:3; 1 Pt 2:5; Jude 20.

Community brought about by the Holy Spirit: Acts 9:31; Rom 15:30; 1 Cor 12:12-13; 2 Cor 3:1-6, 14-16; Eph 2:17-22; 4:1-6; Phil 2:1; Col 1:8; and possibly Acts 5:1-3, 9; 20:28; 2 Cor 13:14; 2 Tm 1:14.

Ministry gifts (charismatic gifts):

The main instructional passages: Rom 12:3-8; 1 Cor 12-14; Eph 4:7-16; 1 Pt 4:10-11.

Other references: Lk 1:14-17; 2:25-32; Acts 6:1-6; 11:22-24; Rom 15:18-19; 1 Cor 2:13; 7:40; Eph 3:4-6, 7; Col 1:28-29; 1 Thes 1:4-5; 1 Tm 4:14; 2 Tm 1:6-9; Heb 2:3-4; 1 Pt 1:10-12; 1 Jn 4:1-6; Rv 19:10; 22:6; and probably 1 Cor 1:4-9; 1 Pt 4:14; and possibly Jn 20:19-25; Jn 14:15-17; 25-27; 15:26-27; 16:7-11; Rom 1:11-12; 1 Cor 2:12; 2 Cor 1:21-22; 6:3-10; Heb 6:4-6. (*Note that these passages only list places where the work of the Holy Spirit is mentioned. There are other passages that speak about the ministries mentioned above.*)

Particular workings of the Spirit (spiritual gifts):

Spiritual gifts: Mt 10:18-20 (Mk 13:11; Lk 12:11-12);
Mk 16:14-20; Acts 1:1-5; 4:8-10; 7:51; 8:26-30, 38-39; 10:19-
20; 11:11-12, 27-28; 13:1-4, 8-12; 16:6-10; 20:22-23; 21:4, 10-
11; 1Cor 2:3-5; 1 Cor 12-14; Gal 3:1-5; Eph 3:4-6;
1 Thes 1:4-5; 5:19-22; 1 Tm 4:1-3; 2 Tm 3:16-17; 2 Pt 1:20-21;
Rv 1:10-11; 2:7, 11, 17, 29; 3:6, 13, 22; 14:13; 17:3; 22:6.
(*Note that most of the ministry gifts mentioned in the New Testament
involve the ability to receive particular workings of the Spirit. Thus the
passages in the section on ministry gifts contain explicit or implicit
references to particular workings of the Spirit.*)

Special fillings of the Spirit: Lk 1:41-42, 67-68; 2:25-29;
Acts 4:23-31; 7:55; 13:52; and possibly Eph 5:18; 1 Pt 4:14.

The Holy Spirit inspiring the Scriptures: Mt 22:43-44
(Mk 12:36); Acts 1:16; 2 Tm 3:16-17; Heb 3:7-9; 9:8; 10:15;
2 Pt 1:20-21, and possibly Eph 6:17. (*Note that to these could be
added the Revelation references under "Particular workings of the
Spirit," since these describe the writing of a book that is in Scripture.*)